THE MASTER'S DECK

THE ULTIMATE PLAYBOOK OF LEARNING AND PLAYING THE GAME OF POWER

by
Terry Triggs

The contents of this work, including, but not limited to, the accuracy of events, people, and places depicted; opinions expressed; permission to use previously published materials included; and any advice given or actions advocated are solely the responsibility of the author, who assumes all liability for said work and indemnifies the publisher against any claims stemming from publication of the work.

All Rights Reserved
Copyright © 2023 by Terry Triggs

No part of this book may be reproduced or transmitted, downloaded, distributed, reverse engineered, or stored in or introduced into any information storage and retrieval system, in any form or by any means, including photocopying and recording, whether electronic or mechanical, now known or hereinafter invented without permission in writing from the publisher.

Dorrance Publishing Co
585 Alpha Drive
Pittsburgh, PA 15238
Visit our website at www.dorrancebookstore.com

ISBN: 978-1-6386-7198-5
eISBN: 978-1-6386-7727-7

Dedication

To my mother and father.
And to all those who strive for greatness.

Acknowledgments

I give all honor and praise to The Creator for blessing me with the ability to share my thoughts in a very special way. I am thankful for too many people to mention. You all know who you are. Each of you has played very important roles in my development. There is also an individual and a source from which, without him or it, I would not have been able to approach this writing project. This school of thought will be readily apparent to those in that sphere. Out of deep respect, I am acknowledging him and that source in this manner.

Introduction

The bulk of the American people have been systematically disempowered, which has led to widespread dissatisfaction with the hand they have been dealt in life. Even so, none of us can just throw our hand in. Who we are is who we are and what we have is what we have. Instead of learning how to master the hand we have been dealt, we go through life dissatisfied, disappointed, and frustrated. Succumbing unwillingly, and often unknowingly to those who have harnessed, to one degree or another, a part of themselves that has equipped them to be the director of their own fate and that of others. We all have voids that needs to be filled and needs that need to be met; and if they remain unfilled and unmet, then we will never be as whole, as complete, or as balanced as we could be.

Knowledge is power, and it is the most essential ingredient you will ever need in life to be successful. Knowledge, and its application is sufficient to get you what you want and need. The alternative, ignorance, is unacceptable, and will only keep you fettered and bound to mediocrity and on the bottom rung of society. It is better to be empowered with knowledge instead.

This book will detail and outline shrewd tactics, seamless strategies, and both concrete and abstract maneuvers. Shrewd tactics in the sense that a peculiar acumenity must be used to produce the desired effect you are after regardless of how it may or may not appear to or affect others. What we are concerned with is not being bound by the thoughts and opinions of others that tends to restrict us. You will always be judged no matter what you do so you might as well do what you want the way you want. The schematics of this must be properly tempered.

By seamless strategies is meant that you should learn and become highly proficient in the use of certain laws, principles, and techniques that will be highlighted in the various cards in this book to the point that they become a natural part of who you are. You will develop a natural remedial response in direct proportion to whatever circumstance you find yourself in. Concrete and abstract maneuvers refer to developing a sophisticated, methodical way of navigating through a multitude of circumstances.

The Master's Deck is comprised of profoundly practical approaches to everyday living situations. The goal, ultimately, is to be able to master any living situation you find yourself in. No more being powerless in these situations. No matter what profession you are in, no matter what manner of education you have, and no matter what walk of life you are from; you will be able to extract something from this book. The varied uses of each card will be determined by you, the reader, in direct proportion to your mental capacity, spiritual depth, and motivating factors.

The 52 cards in this book are divided into four sections so that focalized attention can be given to each law, principle, or concept. However, because certain laws, principles, or concepts overlap in both large and small ways in many of the cards, it is impossible to completely isolate any one of them to one card alone. This is why, although a particular situation may call for this or that card to be played, it just may in fact require a combination or blending of two or more cards. As will be discussed in the fifth section of this book under Winning Hands. At any given time, one particular card may trump all others. The uniqueness of that situation, should it arise, will be made known to you intuitively.

The structure and format of this book is designed to make it a relatively simple read. Terms will be defined to provide meaning and context. Thoughtful questions are presented to stimulate serious thought, answers that provide clear insight, and key points concludes each card to provide easy access to main points.

This writer has no formal training or expertise in any specific field. Yet he has a bevy of personal experience that qualifies him to present to the general public, an inspiring, motivating, enlightening, and edifying compilation of his inner thoughts and viewpoints that he has garnered from his collective experiences. These experiences, in his opinion, transcends ordinary educational norms.

This writer does not propose that he is presenting anything new. Various schools of thought have been amalgamized and modernized to the extent that they can be used more practically in this dispensation of time, which makes this book an invaluable read. This book is in no way intended to be exhaustive. Each topic discussed requires its own book. He is merely touching these points from a uniquely different perspective and manner in concentrated form.

There is a dark side to life that many choose not to acknowledge. In this day and time, you cannot afford to be like the ostrich that sticks its head in the sand ignoring apparent dangerous and problematic conditions, hoping that somehow the dangers and problems will just go away. That is not dealing with reality. The reality of the matter is that this world that we are living in is predominantly dark. Many of our lives have been negatively impacted by this darkness and many of us reflect this darkness in some way.

This does not have to be the case. You can become acquainted with ways to improve your condition. Power has many dynamics and is not always pretty. It has many forms and is not always expressed the same way. It is only when you can harness power that you can effectively change your condition for the better. You cannot be squeamish, morally smug, or self-righteous to enter this realm. Be open-minded and seriously consider what is being presented to you in this book from the unique perspective it is being offered and make it your own. This writer desires that you are profoundly and positively impacted by reading this book and that you come out empowered.

— Terry Triggs

TABLE OF CONTENTS

The Master's Deck: The Ultimate Playbook of Learning & Playing the Game of Power!

Acknowledgments v

Introduction vii

Section I: Spades (Supremacy Clauses) 1
    * Commentary 2
    1. Uncontrolled Emotions 6
    2. Diplomatic Relations 101 10
    3. First Impressions 15
    4. Hidden Plans 20
    5. Necessitated Action 24
    6. Titanic Considerations 29
    7. Knowing People 34
    8. Security Measures 40
    9. The Great Falling Away 45
    10. Sheer Determination 50
    11. Thicker and Blacker 54
    12. Personal Grooming Habits 62
    13. Atmospheric Conditions 67

Section II: Hearts (Power Poses) 75
   * Commentary 76
   14. Chameleonistic Stances 80
   15. Money Matters 84
   16. The Irrevocable Power of Thought 89
   17. Adversarial Companionship 97
   18. Preparing for all Eventualities 102
   19. Insultive Indulgences 106
   20. The Royal Crown Affair 111
   21. The Undeniable Power of Magnetism 115
   22. Team Building 122
   23. Interrogatories 126
   24. The Talking Skull 133
   25. Minimizing Mistakes 137
   26. Total Domination 142

Section III: Clubs (Master Strokes) 147
   * Commentary 148
   27. Remote Control 152
   28. Achilles Heel 158
   29. Ghost Protocol 162
   30. Handling Enemies 169
   31. Fighting Fire with Fire 176
   32. Winning at all Costs 181
   33. Situational Adaptation 187
   34. Beachhead Breaching 191
   35. The Velvet Glove 196
   36. The Trojan Horse 201
   37. Fools Rush in Where Wise Men Fear to Tread 206
   38. The Science of Willing 210
   39. The Thirteenth Chapter 215

Section IV: Diamonds (The Grand Finale) ...221
    * Commentary 222
    40. Appearances 226
    41. The Squeaky Wheel 230
    42. Birds of a Feather 235
    43. The Matter of Trust and the Issue of Loyalty 239
    44. The Gift and the Curse 245
    45. Pyrrhic Victories 251
    46. New Realms of Possibility: 256
    47. Battle Concept 261
    48. Preventive Measures 266
    49. Contractual Obligations 272
    50. Effective Time Management 276
    51. Time, Place, Space Dynamic 281
    52. Modus Operandi 286

Conclusion 291

Bibliography 295

Upcoming Books by the Author 296

SECTION ONE

SPADES

* Commentary I:

What does it mean to be the best and most skilled at what you do? What is the cost of excellence? What makes the great, great? The answers to these questions have a direct bearing on the Supremacy Clause. Each of us have been genetically encoded with this clause. Yet many fall miserably short from their destined greatness. What accounts for this massive downward departure? And what can be done to get you back to where you rightfully belong?

Although the heights and achievements of others are laudable, it is not enough to marvel at their greatness, or their excellence. No. This is nothing but pure laziness. A type of laziness that should be outlawed. Deep down you know that there is much more to you. You can sense it. You can feel it. You know something is missing because there is an emptiness in you that is yearning to be filled with something. But with what? Not knowing what, you continue to be weighed down by ignorance and inertia. A weight that is easier to succumb to rather than fight your way from up under. You must have an epiphany type experience where one day you decide enough is enough. When you say to yourself that you are not satisfied with where you are in life and that you are going to do whatever it takes, for however long it takes, to change the reality of your life.

The Master's Deck

You have to go to a special place in your mind that you had no idea it existed until you forged your way into it. But once you get there, whoa. Nothing is greater than when you can tap into a source of power from within that is so overwhelming that it alters your entire being. A higher state of consciousness has been exposed to you and now you begin to operate on a higher level of thought. Invariably you think differently. You move differently. You move with purpose. You are focused. You have a greater sense of awareness. You have discovered something great within yourself. However, discovery alone is insufficient. It is only a starting point. Now is where the real work begins.

You are the first one on the scene to witness this wonder. This is why it is said that the truly great ones know of their greatness long before others do. All it took was a glimpse, a mere morsel to get you going. Now you want more. You become filled with an unquenchable desire to excel; to succeed. This desire fuels you and thrusts you in the direction of the fulfillment of your desires. This is what enables you to endure all the pain and suffering associated with becoming great, excelling in something, and being the best. You are comforted every step of the way even though this is one of the most difficult journeys you will ever have to take in your life. You are all alone. But guess what? It couldn't happen any other way. Such is the price to be paid.

Excellence requires tremendous sacrifice, the ability to surmount blocks of pain, and being able to overcome rejection and setbacks. So, how much are you willing to sacrifice? How much are you willing to endure? And will you stay the course in the face of vehement opposition? Only you can answer these questions. To be the best in anything means you have to put in the time and the work. You can never rest on your laurels, at any point. You must hone your skills at every available opportunity.

Ultimately what you get in the end is not only what you put in, but what you are ready to receive and use. This is nature's own ecosystem working right inside of you. Abundance is already in you, but it is given to you under the specified conditions just spoken of. Brace yourself because this is where things get a little rough. It doesn't really matter because you are built for this. If you were not, then you would have never been granted access. Endure and enjoy.

(Supremacy Clauses)

Cards 1 - 13:

1. Uncontrolled Emotions; 2. Diplomatic Relations 101; 3. First Impressions; 4. Hidden Plans; 5. Necessitated Actions; 6. Titanic Considerations; 7. Knowing People; 8. Security Measures; 9. The Great Falling Away; 10. Sheer Determination; 11. Thicker and Blacker; 12. Personal Grooming Habits; 13. Atmospheric Conditions

Card 1: Uncontrolled Emotions

Uncontrolled - Free from control by a superior power. Incapable of being controlled. Ungovernable.

Control - To exercise directing influence over. To regulate. To have power over.

Emotion - An affective state of consciousness where you experience anger, sadness, fear, etc. which is distinguished from volitional states of consciousness. Intense feelings.

* Concept/Objective: To highlight that part of yourself that needs to be brought under your control, why you should do it, and how to do it. If not, you will never get off the ground floor of power.

(Questions)
1. What is power's most crucial foundation? And why?
2. In what way do uncontrolled emotions produce blind spots in you?
3. Can emotions, on their own, get you what you want and/or need in life?

Of all the foundations upon which power is built, being able to control your emotions is the most crucial. The very powerful obtained their power through machinations that the general public would shudder at. Decisions made with nothing but pure intellect and stone-cold logic without regard for how those decisions may personally affect others is something that many cannot do. The compartmentalization of your emotions is key here. Thinking of nothing but accomplishing your goals.

There is no good that can come from uncontrolled emotions. It is power's greatest impediment and must be properly harnessed, controlled, and directed. If not, then mediocrity, at best, will forever be your lot. A lot of elaboration is not really necessary. History is replete with examples of those who have fallen, experienced a loss, or brought upon themselves unfavorable consequences because of not being able to control their emotional response in a given situation. Emotional turbulence produces in the mind "blind spots" that cause you to misperceive reality. Causing you to make missteps and mistakes. This can be very detrimental.

The ability to control your emotions is an indispensable art that must be tended to. This, for most of us, is not an easy feat. However, what worthwhile endeavor is? Ignoring this part of yourself will only keep you in a disadvantaged, subservient, and powerless position. Human beings are generally controlled by their emotions. Whichever way their emotions go so will they. But this does not have to be the case. Different emotions put you in different moods. And usually the mood of the moment affects your decision-making. It can be very dangerous to make emotional decisions. Not to mention the possible unfavorable effects that flow forth from such decisions.

Fear restricts. It will cause you to be overly hesitant. Even to the point of non-action. Love, not properly tempered, will cause you to be too empathetic, and excessive tenderness of heart gives rise to weak decisions. Anger is a very blinding and potentially destructive emotion. You must become acutely aware of your emotional make-up and tendencies. Don't be irresponsible. Overcome your fears. Temper your love. Control your anger.

There are occasions when emotions can serve to fuel you. However, it must be done in such a way where you don't allow yourself to be consumed in the process. One of the best portraits to illustrate this point is when Moses met Jehovah at the Burning Bush. The bush was on fire, being emblematic of God's anger. Two key points; first, His anger was justified. Secondly, His anger was controlled. Emotions interrupt our ability to think and see things as they are. It takes great discipline to be able to think through anger. Absent your ability to do that, there is never a justifiable reason to respond to a situation in a state of rage. Damage done from anger can be irreparable and irreversible.

Greed opens you up to be deceived. It has also been known to produce a treacherous state of mind in the beholder. This mindset carries with it seeds of betrayal that make it hard for the one who is

The Master's Deck

greedy to resist the ploys of others. Lust is an inordinate appetite for something or someone. This inordinacy causes you to be blind to everything around you except the object of your lusts. Hate is an intense emotion that is the engine behind many thoughtless, unjustifiable, and unnecessary actions that thwarts you from reaching your overall goals and objectives. Reflect over greed, lust, and hate and how they must be effectively dealt with.

Master your emotions. In doing so, you have established power's most crucial foundation and you are well on your way to limitless power. With the above mentioned emotions under control, along with a plethora of others, the progress you can make will be unlimited. All emotions apply. Be careful of those who you surround yourself with who have yet to attain the level of discipline and mastery you have emotionally. For, if emotions, for the most part, controls man; then you can be controlled by another person's emotions vicariously in said manner.

Certain emotions are necessary to overcome because they can literally stifle you. And anything that serves as an impediment or is in the pathway of you reaching your goals must be relentlessly attacked. If not, you are susceptible to being frozen in time. Immobility is certain death. Live.

Emotionalism alone should never be relied upon to get you what you desire. Remember, emotions cloud your judgment. Practice patience when you sense yourself losing it. Reel things back in. Wait. Then reapproach when you've had a chance to reassess. Use logic. Calculate. Once this is done, then move, and let the chips fall where they may.

* Key Points:
   a. Never take anything personally
   b. Isolate your emotions
   c. Be patient until certain feelings subside before making decisions
   d. Don't be controlled by another's emotional instability
   e. Carefully controlled emotions can serve as an impetus to propel you forward
   f. A powerful foundation is built upon your ability to control your emotions
   g. Different emotions produce different moods

Card 2: Diplomatic Relations 101

Diplomacy - Skill in handling affairs without arousing hostility.

Relation - A state of affairs existing between those having dealings.

* Concept/Objective: Develop good social skills. Use tact. Understand individuals' psychological make-up. Arm yourself with these and you'll be able to deal successfully with an array of people from all walks of life. Don't, and you will be ineffective when dealing with people and potential disasters won't be averted.

(Questions)
1. Why are diplomatic relations important?
2. What does it take to be a world-class statesman?
3. When diplomatic talks prove unsuccessful, what is the next course of action?

Diplomacy is a science that deals with peculiar relationships between peoples or nations. Especially as it relates to sensitive and delicate matters. Or even if it's just the advancement of a cause, an agenda, or some other interest. Diplomats are highly skilled in the art of negotiation. He is a high level negotiator. Everyone is not capable of being tactful in stressful situations. Diplomats are.

So the use of appropriate and specific language that is designed to influence the other party to agree to a set of terms even though those terms may not be completely in the other party's favor takes an amazing ability. By so much being at stake, it takes a special individual to be a diplomat. One who has good people skills, is able to convey ideas clearly, and understands the psychological make-up of people.

A diplomat never utters as much as a word or as little as a syllable without first running it over in his mind. He is careful as he uses his abilities to promote his agenda and protect himself and the interests he represents from non-compliant parties. Tensions can run high. To be able to lessen tensions takes a premiere diplomat. And a premiere diplomat is a world-class statesman. If it wasn't for a diplomats effectiveness in handling potentially volatile situations, then more wars and hostile relations would exist. So their importance cannot be overstated.

Even on an individual basis, which is what were after here, you should develop the necessary diplomatic skills that would allow you to masterfully deal with situations that require a sober approach. This will carry you much further than having to resort to violence or aggression in handling affairs. For that has its place.

"A man who knows the court is master of his gestures, of his eyes and of his face; he is profound, impenetrable; he dissimulates bad offices, smiles at his enemies, controls his irritation, disguises his passions, belies his heart, speaks and acts against his feelings." 2

This is what it takes to be a world-class statesman. You have to embody and supremely practice every aspect of the above to perfection. Think about it, your eyes, your face, and your gestures are very revealing and can convey a message often more effectively than words can. Your words may say one thing, but you can contradict those words or give mixed messages through unconscious physical cues.

His intellectual depth, and impenetrability is top tier. How cunning do you have to be to divert the attention of a person so far away from what is really in your mind? And to have enough self-control and discipline to smile in the face of your enemies? That's not easy. But it is when you are able to detach yourself from the situation keeping the larger objective in mind. All the while things may be said or conditions may exist that really get under his skin, but guess what?, he can't show it, and he doesn't. He controls his irritation like no other. You too must do the same.

Now comes the ability to use the art of misdirection. Never letting others know what you are up to. Not showing the true intentions of what is in your heart. Ending it with the creme de le creme of moves which is to be able to muster up the wherewithal to speak in such strong and convincing terms that go against what you actually feel. And your actions mirror this sentiment exactly. If that isn't world-class, then I don't know what is. This arsenal from which a diplomat operates is indispensable. Make these abilities a part of your repertoire if your desire is to be of the elite in the realm of power.

The diplomatic approach is an ordinary course of action that is designed to facilitate good relations in a non-combative way. The goal is to lessen the tensions in highly combustible situations. Sometimes diplomatic talks stall. More than one session is sometimes needed. Especially depending upon the severity of the issue at hand. You have to take into consideration the history between the parties involved. You must factor in the reasonableness of the offered terms. When this process is exhausted and has run its course, then other measures must be utilized to make the other capitulate.

Give the diplomatic process a legitimate try because of its importance in maintaining peaceful relations. Learn how to be subtle when it is needed and learn the more direct approach casting subtlety aside. Be charming and manipulative at the same time. Seduce and persuade. Learn as much about your target or counterpart as possible. Knowing what makes the other tick is a lever that can be used to push and prod others in the direction of your choosing.

This process is more mental than anything else. It is all about connecting with people where it matters most, in the heart and mind, and using that to accomplish your goals and objectives. The diplomatic craft requires a high skill set in subtlety, misdirection, and dealing with people.

"It is better to win hearts, than cities, better to battle with hearts than with weapons." [1]

* **Key Points:**
    a. Diplomats are high level negotiators
    b. Being tactful is important in diplomatic matters

c. Develop the right arsenal in order to be a world-class statesman
d. Keep the larger goal in mind
e. Be patient with the diplomatic process
f. When all else fails, do whatever is necessary

Card 3: First Impressions

First - Preceding all others in time, order, or importance. Something that is first. Initial.

Impression - The effect produced by impressing.

* Concept/Objective: First impressions greatly influence subsequent interactions. Leave nothing to chance. When making your mark on someone make it count. Always put your best foot forward and your next step will naturally follow suit.

(Questions)

1. What are you best known for?
2. What would you rather deal with, a bad conscience or a bad reputation?
3. What is the science behind the power of introductions?

"The first impression that one gets from a ruler and of his intelligence is from seeing the men that he has about him. When they are competent and faithful, he can always be considered wise, as he has been able to recognize ability and keep them faithful." 7

You should be known for things that enhance

your standing in the eyes of the people. The most important time to create an enduring and impactful impression is when you first meet someone, or during the initial phase of the relationship. Whatever it is, it must be something outstanding. You could be known for your unquestioned honesty, your exceptional brilliance, or even your charitable spirit. Any of these will firmly establish you in the minds of others in ways that can only benefit you in future dealings. You don't have to be known for something good necessarily, as long as whatever it is, it can somehow serve you in some capacity.

There was a commercial that said, 'Image is nothing, thirst is everything.' Their aim was to sell a product, not the truth. The truth is, it should matter to you how you are perceived by others. Another's perception of you can carry you a long way or it can also serve as a hindrance. The eye of the onlooker is a powerful tool that must not be ignored. Just ask those who have been at the wrong end of eyewitness testimony. The ever probing eye sees images, not thirst, and that which is seen is all that matters.

You live in a world with billions of people. How any of them view you will determine how they deal with you. Don't misconstrue this, I'm not saying that you should appease anyone, never that, but what I am saying is that you should develop the necessary people skills that will equip you to have successful relations with others. You will always have to deal with people from both ends of the spectrum and all in between. Why not take the time it takes to understand the minds of men. Ignoring others' psychological make-up is unwise. If you lived in a bubble it wouldn't matter, but you don't, so it should.

Never live your life according to the whims and wishes of others. You shouldn't even try to. At the same time you must not underestimate the power of first impressions and how they greatly affect every ensuing encounter after that. Remember your goal; to master any and all living situations. Keep this theme in mind as you proceed through each card. This context is necessary so things can be seen in the proper perspective.

"Since we must live in society and must depend on the opinions of others, there is nothing to be gained by neglecting your reputation."   2

In the realm of power, your reputation is undoubtedly more important than your conscience. A bad reputation is hard to recover from. A bad conscience, through certain penances, and over time, can be alleviated. A bad reputation is visible to all. A bad conscience is visible only to yourself. Not many see how you think or how you feel, but everyone sees you as you appear to be or what you are known for.

The above question number two involves the

staining of your reputation. Having a bad reputation strips you of your power in a lot of ways, therefore, it must be protected at all costs. The extent to which you go to protect your good name can extend far beyond what is considered normal. A bad act, which can torment your conscience, is far better than a bad act, that can ruin or damage your reputation. Do whatever you have to do to clean your reputation up. As for me, I would rather live with a bad conscience than with a bad reputation. The former is easier to cope with.

Lastly, allow me to touch on the power of introductions and why you should be ever so attentive to them. How you introduce yourself, how someone else introduces you, or how you introduce others is very important. Each of these have their own significance. All of this is connected with first impressions as they relate to your reputation. Don't introduce just anyone into certain circles. By doing so you are vouching for them. This cosigning can come back to hurt you if that person you introduced turns out to be sour.

At the same time, never let someone who is not highly regarded introduce you into certain circles. Their low standing will be indirectly cast upon you. Distant introductions apply as well. Your physical presence is not even required to be introduced to others. How someone introduces you in your absence can affect how you are introduced and received in the future, in person, which is based on your reputation. The point is that you should not underestimate the power of introductions and what they impress upon others.

"...a man who performed an introduction was thereafter responsible for the actions of the man he introduced. It was common that a man would pay with his life and the lives of his family for the misconduct of someone he had introduced. You will forever be marked by the man who performs your introductions...if he is known and respected by those you meet, you will share in his good reputation."[6]

* **Key Points:**
    a. The most important time to create an impactful and enduring impression is during initial encounters
    b. Establish a reputation for some outstanding quality
    c. Develop the necessary people skills that will equip you to have successful relations with others
    d. A bad conscience is better than a bad reputation
    e. Never underestimate the power of introductions

Card 4: Hidden Plans

Hidden - Being out of sight or not readily apparent: Concealed. Obscure, Unexplained, Undisclosed, Unknown.

Plan - A method for achieving an end.

* Concept/Objective: People who tell all their business have no business. There is nothing that can be gained from exposing the inner workings of your plans to anyone. Other than to satisfy some insecurity within yourself. But at what expense? The guiding rule is that everything should be on a need-to-know basis. Trust only yourself with your plans.

(Questions)

1. What are the most important tools in serious planning?
2. Why must brilliant plans be kept hidden?
3. Is there ever an occasion when the inner workings of your planning is exposed to anyone? And if so, to what extent?

"Leaders plan in the beginning when they do things."[1]

Secrecy is the most important tool in serious planning. The idea is to ensure that your most sensitive secrets remain just that, secret. There is nothing more promising than a well thought out plan. And there is nothing more problematic than having that plan leaked. When you are serious about your business, and your business is serious, why wouldn't you want to make certain that your business is protected from any outside influences?

There is just simply too much that can go wrong when someone is in possession of vital information unnecessarily. Don't let an inflated ego or an undisciplined tongue cause you to want to share matters of importance. Only more harm than good can come out of being so loose with your business affairs. Keep things sealed.

The second most important tool in serious planning is serious planning. The mental energy needed for in depth planning demands focalized attention. This means distractions should be at a minimum. Details are important. One unaccounted for thing can throw everything off. So much thought should accompany your planning that it covers any foreseeable pitfall or obstacle.

In the very beginning, you should be able to see the end result of your planning. Having alternative approaches ready as a result of your calculations, enhances your success rate. You have to look at business as a form of warfare, and no general in his right mind will make his battle plans known to his adversaries. You shouldn't either.

The third most important tool in serious planning involves the caliber of people with whom you do business. This is perhaps one of the most overlooked aspects of doing good business. This cannot be stressed enough. How do you determine who is a viable candidate to do business with? Keep in mind the principles of knowing people in card seven. You will never be able to fully know for certain, but you can come as close as humanly possible.

When someone shows you something not right, no matter how small it is, heed it. If you get a bad feeling or bad vibe about something, withdraw. Never let the prospect of gain cause you to look past what you see or what you feel. Greed is dangerous and can blind you to glaring red flags. Don't be blindly ambitious. Use reason and logic.

History is full of lessons of why your future greatness should be made known to no one no matter how close they are to you. There are so many variables that can interfere with your plans that you cannot afford to leave anything to chance. Isaac wisely instructed his son Jacob not to tell his vision to no man. Not even his brothers. Had he listened, he would have spared himself from being the recipient of envy, jealousy and a treacherous plot.

Besides that, why subjugate yourself to the judgements of petty minds. People will find any number of reasons to find something wrong with what you set out to do. The best remedy for that is to keep people in the dark. Why even bother putting yourself in that predicament? You don't have to explain yourself to anyone. When it is all said and done, the only person that matters is you.

Don't let guilt or anything else get in your way. And don't concern yourself with nosey people, they are everywhere. Only let them see what you want them to see. Misdirect if you have to.

There is a certain part of you that should be reserved just for you. Don't be an open book. Be mysterious without coming off as suspicious. Because when others know you are up to something and they can't figure it or you out, they become suspicious. And suspicion can lead to an interference that you just don't need.

However, there will be times when the inner workings of your planning is exposed to others. Two conditions must be met for this to happen, and a third point if the first two apply. First, they must be a part of the plan. Secondly, only if the exposure is somehow beneficial in the fulfillment of the plan. The third point being that if you have to reveal something to a participant, only reveal what is necessary for the second conditional point, nothing more.

Remember, everything is on a need-to-know basis. If they don't need to know, then they need not know. Don't deviate from this law no matter what and you have successfully controlled the parameters of your plans to the extent that you are able to.

Your plans should not be on display for all to see. At least not your real plans. Good plans are the cornerstone to building something substantial. And good planning is full of insightful considerations which makes making bad moves a rare thing. If you ever have to look at something from hindsight because of a mistake, then you somehow failed to fully use each tool in serious planning.

Lastly, aside from not divulging what your plans are, equally important is not revealing the timing of your plans. In other words, the what and the when should only be known by you. Of all plans, hidden ones are the best.

* Key Points:
  a. Secrecy is the most important tool in serious planning
  b. Everything is on a need-to-know basis
  c. Serious planning is serious business and should be taken as such
  d. Only do business with high caliber people
  e. Plan all the way to the end

Card 5: Necessitated Action

Necessary - Absolutely needed. Required. Logically unavoided.

Action - A thing done. An undertaking. Enterprise. Initiative.

* Concept/Objective: Every action has an equal and opposite reaction. Control the action and you control the reaction. Every action must be governed by

necessity. Avoid unnecessary actions. Never get induced to act by others. Move on your own terms.

(Questions)
1. What is the law of necessity?
2. What possible consequences do you open yourself up to when your actions are unnecessary?
3. Are there any circumstances when non-action is the best course of action?

The law of necessity states that if something is not necessary for you to do or say, then it is absolutely necessary that you don't do it or say it. This law should be used as a guiding principal that guides you in everything. You can never go wrong when you are compelled by necessity to act in a certain way. Act only if you have to. Act only when you are prepared to. And act only if you can win. If not, desist. Unnecessary actions bring unnecessary problems.

By staying within the bounds of necessity you protect yourself from any number of consequences. A lot of unnecessary problems that many suffer from could have been avoided had they been more aware of their actions. Don't be so ignorant of how connected your actions are and the effect they have on your life.

The law of cause and effect is an unending series of events and circumstances that are spawned from each other in turn. They are cyclical. There is no such thing as a chance happening. If something happened it was the result of something real. Knowing this you must never attribute what happens to you from others as something that just happened.

Equally, you must be conscious of every move you make and what those moves produce. All it takes is one errant move. A move that may seem insignificant to you. But as will be repeatedly advocated in this book, it is always the smallest things that make the biggest difference. When you fail to make conscious and deliberate moves, then you are subjecting yourself to forces outside of your control.

You had better recognize the seriousness of this point before you dig a hole for yourself that is easy to get in but hard to get out. Thoughtless actions can be costly. Never engage in any act without considering the consequences of those actions first.

One of the most important things to consider when it comes to necessitated action is when you are able to have control over the when, the where, and the how. If you can dictate the timing of your actions, the place of your actions, and the methodology of what you do, then you increase your chances of success in that action. But when you are forced to move at the behest of others at a time not of your choosing, at a location not of your choosing, and in a manner you are unaccustomed to, then you are at a decided disadvantage.

Even to the dismay of others, it then becomes necessary for you to regain the initiative to act when, where, and how you want to and you must make sure these factors exist for you. There is no law governing how you arrive at this point. The only law is that of necessity. And necessity knows no law. It is a law unto itself.

Sometimes no action is the best course of action. You have to learn how to sniff out the right moment to move and the right moment not to move. If it is not right, then be still. Exercise patience. Wait for the right moment. It takes great effort not to move when you want to. But you have to ask yourself, despite wanting to move, do you have to? If not, then don't.

This in and of itself is action clothed in non-action. When you can do this, you have mastered a very critical art. You are now exercising control over your movements instead of aimlessly moving about from one place to another. But once you notice a shift and it signals you to act, then move out at once. Some benefits are temporal and can only be seized upon within a certain time frame. Things not swiftly acted upon can get lost. This is different than inaction based on ignorance or fear. Which is an altogether different thing.

The most important thing to keep in mind is that there is an aim and a purpose for everyone and everything. Once you discover yours, then it will provide you with the much needed guidance for the course of your life. Now when you involve yourself in any undertaking, hopefully it will be towards the fulfillment of your life's purpose. And any action that can lead you in this direction is a necessary action.

Never impose upon others what you think they should be doing, unless it is necessary. A different course has been carved out for them. Is it necessary to tell whoever what you think they should be doing? Your child perhaps. But beyond that, a degree of latitude must be extended to others to find their way.

Along the way they may act in a way that from your vantage point is aimless, nonproductive, or even harmful; in which cases you should let the overall circumstances and your relationship with that person dictate to what extent you infringe upon their life. Don't force things. Let it be a natural matter of course. You'd be amazed how much can be thrown off by forced action that goes against nature. Read the situation for what it is.

As I conclude this card I strongly urge you to reflect over the fact that aggression does not equate to effective action. Although at times it can. What you are after is results. Results are all that matter. This is how you measure the effectiveness of your actions. When you move based upon the law of necessity you can never go wrong. You can never lose even if you do lose, why, because you had to move.

* **Key Points:**
   a. Unnecessary actions bring unnecessary problems
   b. Purposeful non-action is action
   c. Always consider consequences
   d. Never go beyond what is necessary
   e. Necessity knows no law
   f. Aggressive action does not equate to effective action

Card 6: Titanic Considerations

Titanic - Having great magnitude, force, or power: Colossal.

Consider - To think about carefully. To take into account. To give thought to in order to reach a suitable decision.

* Concept/Objective: The basic idea here is to strongly consider various factors that could greatly impact your life in a negative way. Your involvement in any affair, directly or otherwise, if it can harm you in any way, must be strongly considered by you. This consideration will let you know whether to proceed further or to withdraw yourself completely.

(Questions)
1. How can you tell if something or someone is doomed to fail?
2. What types of considerations must be a part of the process of determining the potential colossal

effects of an undertaking?
3. What is the greatest benefit from 'considering' titanic happenings?

This card can be considered the cousin of card eighteen, yet it has its own distinctive qualities. There is a basic premise that is often underrated, but yet it is a simple one that can protect you from a lot of trouble before it happens, and that is to always consider the consequences of your actions. How many times have you disregarded the consequences of your actions only to suffer as a result? This card is designed to assist you and to prevent you from looking back after the fact on what you should have done.

Sometimes you won't be able to foresee the doom of an undertaking, the failure of an operation, or the bad ending of a particular endeavor, but you can know of its possibility based upon wise considerations of the undertaking, the operation, or the endeavor. Ask yourself, what can go wrong? Whatever can go wrong has to be considered. Based upon those considerations, better decisions can be made and disasters averted.

"If people do not consider what is remote, they will have trouble near at hand...educated people think without leaving their positions. Thinking means correct strategy, consideration means thinking of plans for eventualities...therefore if you want to think of the advantages in a situation, it is imperative to consider the harm; if you want to think about success, it is imperative to consider failure."1

There will always be risk factors involved with anything. Some risks will be greater than others. The key will be in your risk assessment abilities. This is what you are doing when you consider things. You are merely assessing things along certain lines. This will allow you to determine the inherent benefits and harms of something or someone. Your thinking should be focused on the task at hand, while at the same time considering distant ramifications. All risks must be assessed no matter how small. Small things have a way of making the biggest difference.

Everything conceivable by you must be considered. It is not easy to consider that which you have no knowledge of. Some things can only be known after the fact. By then it would be too late though. Because of this, the least you can do is gather as much information as possible so that your considerations can be that much broader and yield greater results.

How many times have you done something that didn't quite turn out right and it cost you in the end? After the fact you ask yourself, "why didn't I follow my first mind?" or, "why didn't I think of that?" Had you taken the time necessary to consider things, perhaps you would have made a better decision. The point is, and all I have been attempting to say all along is, always think before you act, weigh your options, and consider great things.

The greatest benefit from 'considering' great things is that it can alleviate mistakes. One less mistake is better than one more. You will move more wisely and possess a God like ability that will cause others to wonder how, in what way, do you not fall victim to things that most others fall victim to? It will because you believe something, know something, and are practicing something that others don't believe, don't know, and aren't practicing.

You benefit by being able to predict misfortune before it happens by anticipating, calculating, and deducing. You will be able to avoid high risk people. People who are known or prone to get into trouble easily. People who, whenever they come around, something always seems to go wrong. They are simply unlucky. Negative. Unhappy. From such, stay far away. Whatever the case, there will always be indicators. When things don't look right, keep your distance. When things don't feel right, keep your distance.

Why distance yourself from things or people that you see as toxic, hazardous, or combustible? Your proximity to what is called ground zero will cause you to suffer a similar fate as if you were right smack dab in the middle of the action. You don't have to look any further than the Titanic ship that sank on its maiden voyage. The sheer size and weight of that ship, when it sank, caused any object within a considerable distance from it to sink also.

That is how strong the gravitational pull was to draw objects into its inescapable grasp. And this is why you must consider things that are of titanic proportions. Which is anything important. I hope this makes it crystal clear why you should stay clear and far away from anything and anyone that can bring you down or cause you to go down with it. These types of considerations are to your advantage. And not to consider them are to your detriment.

"Enlightened people know the obvious when they see the subtle, know the end when they see the beginning, thus there is no way for disaster to happen. This is due to thoughtful consideration." [1]

* **Key Points:**
- a. Always consider the consequences of your actions
- b. Don't participate in anything that can take you away from your goal
- c. Assess risk factors to determine inherent benefits or harms
- d. Always think before you act
- e. Keep your distance when things don't look right

f. Keep your distance when things don't feel right

Card 7: Knowing People
Knowledge - The fact or condition of knowing someone with familiarity gained through association. To be aware of. To become acquainted with certain facts or truths about someone.

People - Human beings. Persons.

* Concept/Objective: Don't be fooled by how people represent themselves to you. Most people have layers upon layers covering them that conceal the essence of who they really are. It is in peeling these layers back that reveals people for who and what they are. A revelation that may even shock you.

(Questions)
1. Why is knowing others important?
2. In what way can you cause someone to reveal themselves to you without their consent or knowledge?
3. Of all the people you should know, who should be uppermost?

The ability to know who you are dealing with is difficult, but not impossible. By being around someone for long periods of time we may assume we know them. This is a natural assumption. An unwise one nonetheless. Depending upon the circumstances of the relationship this assumption can be harmless. On the other hand not so much. On the surface of things it should be of no surprise that it takes time to get to know people. Gradually things about others are made known to us.

What we are after here is in uncovering those who attempt to deceive you into thinking you are dealing with a sheep, but in reality, you have been dealing with a wolf all along. This may seem like an extreme reference but you'd be surprised of the level of deception from which people operate. Either way, you always want to know who you are dealing with. And this is why it is important to know others.

Now, obviously there are differences between what we display in public as opposed to our private life. Like home and work. But a person's authentic self should be noticeable in varying degrees in both settings. And what we shield from others in certain settings is to be expected and proportionate to that setting.

Just think for a minute now about the people you know. Now ask yourself, how much do you really know about them? How much should you expect to know of others? How much you expect to know should be determined by the type of relationship you and the other person have.

The hardest thing for many to understand is when they think they know someone, then all of a sudden the other person exposes a side of themselves that is least expected. We accuse the person of changing up on us. I'm sure this has happened to you on occasion. Don't be perplexed because the bulk of a person's true identity is always hidden from you upon initial encounters. Besides, we all have more than one side, but what side comes out is based upon the occasion or circumstance.

Being able to control a set of circumstances can allow you to cause others to expose a part of themselves that they would rather you did not know or see. Circumstances are revealing factors because more often than not a person does not know who they are or what they are going to do until they find themselves in a particular circumstance. Sometimes you don't even know yourself until you have been tested by a particular circumstance. Things will come up out of you that may even shock and surprise you.

The point is, either end on the spectrum of characteristics will come out based upon what the circumstances are and who the individual is. This includes but is not limited to bravery or cowardice, faithfulness or unfaithfulness, honesty or shystiness, chasteness and virtue or lasciviousness, and so on. In other words there is much underneath the surface that needs to be factored in when dealing with anyone.

Knowing yourself is essential. There is a common thread that connects all people. To know yourself is to know others. The Art of War states that one who knows only himself is assured of victory half of the time; one who knows only the enemy is assured of victory half of the time. But one who knows himself and his enemy is assured of victory every time.

It is for this reason you should never ignore the hearts and minds of others. How they think. How they feel. What makes them tick. No subtle cue should be ignored. People are always exposing themselves on a subconscious level. How someone walks, contorts their face, or even chews their food are points of identification.

The range of people who you will encounter in life will be wide and varied. However, there are types. Meaning, you will be able to identify a trait or characteristic that serves as an indicator to the type of person you are dealing with. Even if you have never met this person before. There is just something about them that reminds you of someone you do or did know. This is because of the great similarities between people. If you have dealt with a petty person before let's say for example, then there will be a certain trait that characterizes that person. This same trait can be found in perhaps millions of people. So it's not hard to see people before they actually come.

Things change all the time. People do too. You

should make it a regular practice to constantly reassess everyone that you come in contact with. Who knows what could have transpired between your last encounter that puts someone else in a different spirit or energy. A spirit or energy that can potentially be harmful to you. Even if not harmful, you still will want to know how to handle any change that has taken place with anyone you deal with. This will enable you to promote more harmonious relationships with others.

This particular insight and practice will put you in a superior position when it comes to dealing with people based upon your understanding of people. This assessment can be done visually for the most part because their face will be the most visible sign of what is going on. Knowing people entails becoming knowledgeable of the nature of human beings. Knowing the nature of people puts you in a much better position to effectively deal with any person you come in contact with.

"Nothing is harder to see into than people's natures. Though good and bad are different, their conditions and appearances are not always uniform. There are some people who are nice enough but steal. Some people are outwardly respectful while inwardly making fools of everyone. Some people are brave on the outside yet cowardly on the inside. Some people do their best but are not loyal." [1]

What can be gathered here is that you should

look for contrasts. Usually someone who is so adamant and pronounced about something and they overly parade the fact that they are this or that, then maybe they are trying hard to cover up the fact that they are in fact the very opposite.

A person who tries to flaunt their honesty all out of proportion, may really be a crook. A person who professes their loyalty more with their words than with their actions, might be hiding the fact that they are really only loyal to themselves and their own personal agenda. And so on.

There are very specific techniques to employ that allows you to observe a person's ideas, how people change, how perceptive people are, gauge their braveness, see into their nature, measure their modesty, and to check their trustworthiness.

"First is to question them concerning right and wrong, to observe their ideas.

Second is to exhaust all their arguments, to see how they change.

Third is to consult with them about strategy, to see how perceptive they are.

Fourth is to announce that there is trouble, to see how brave they are.

Fifth is to get them drunk to observe their nature.

Sixth is to present them with the prospect of gain, to see how modest they are.

Seventh is to give them a task to do within a

specific time, to see how trustworthy they are." 1

These are but a few ways to see into people to be able to know who you are dealing with. The goal is to always know more about others than they know about you. There is nothing to be gained by not knowing others. Knowing people is a major proponent in the realm of power because in the realm of power you have to deal with people. And nothing is considered more clumsy than dealing with people you know absolutely nothing about.

* Key Points:
    a. Never assume you know someone just because you associate with them
    b. The bulk of a person's true identity is always hidden from your view upon initial encounters
    c. Circumstances have a way of revealing others to you; yourself included
    d. Never ignore the hearts and minds of others
    e. People change
    f. Learn the nature of people

Card 8: Security Measures

Security - To be free from danger. The quality or state of being secure.

Measure - To choose or control with cautious restraint. To regulate by a standard.

   * Concept/Objective: Adhering to a good security

protocol will protect you from dangers both known and unknown. Seen and unseen. Small and great. Any deviation will open you up to possible harm. Stay disciplined and diligent. Always remember, safety first.

(Questions)
1. Why should security be a top priority for you?
2. What measures can be taken to ensure your safety?
3. What are some examples of great security risks?

There are countless dangers in the world that lurk behind every corner. Dangers that on the surface appear to be innocuous. And yet, it is these types of dangers that can harm you the most. At least open dangers present you with the opportunity to take the necessary precautions to protect yourself. This is not the case with disguised, hidden, and unseen dangers. This makes it necessary to formulate security measures to ensure your overall safety. Formulation alone is not enough. You must be found continuously following these measures. Any deviation makes you susceptible to attack. All it takes is one lapse in security to render you a consequence that there is no coming back from.

The essence of your own personal security lies in your ability to be security minded at all times. Never be caught unaware. Being aware of your surroundings is a good starting point. Be aware of subtleties. Anything that is out of place or out of the ordinary are signs of potential harm. These small shifts should trigger in you a more heightened awareness and preparedness. The more you know of a potential threat enables you to establish concrete measures. Beyond that, most everything up to that point is general and basic.

Surely danger exists in the foods you eat. The air you breathe. The water you drink. Certain hygiene products. Traveling. Sports. And a host of other things. Our primary focus here is securing your person from being harmed by other people. You are your own best defense against any would-be attacker. By taking personal control of your life and not having it completely in the hands of and in the control of others limits dangerous situations. No one is going to protect you and your interests better than you.

Measure one is to take charge. Once you take charge; measure two is to be alert to all within your range of sight and hearing. No matter where you are or what you are doing never become so absorbed or preoccupied in that place or in that activity that it puts blinders on your eyes or covers over your ears. You'd be surprised how effective just these two measures are when it comes to detection and prevention. The greater the security concern, the greater the parameters taken to combat those   concerns. Canvass all possible threats.

Whoever can harm you or whatever can go wrong will dictate for you what measure to take. Every situation is uniquely different and calls for very specific tailor made measures.

Whatever you do, you must be thorough. Thoroughness in security is a broad concept that covers a multitude of measures. Evasion is a measure that is a simple yet effective way to expose potential threats and thwart would-be attacks. When driving, for example, from one place to another, make it a habit to observe those in your rearview to see if you are being followed. This is harder to detect on straightaways unless you are highly trained. Making several turns is easier to detect if you are being followed if you are a novice.

There are instances when the same car is noticed on several separate occasions. If there is a great distance to be traveled regularly by you from a known location to an unknown location, let's say from work to home, then you can be spot followed over a protracted period of time. Meaning, if it can be determined that you travel the same way every day, then you don't have to be followed all at once. It can be broken up over several days until your final destination is known.

The only defense against this is to not become predictable. Predictability is dangerous. Predictability is a perpetrator's greatest weapon that he uses against you. When your movements are known in advance it puts you at greater risk. More planning can be done from a perpetrator that helps him carry out his mission that much more easily. By occasionally switching your routes you can thwart or at least make things more difficult. The above example may seem extreme for some. For others they are well aware of this practice. This is what I mean when I say be thorough, even though this is only one example.

Gas stations are hotspots as well. Carjackings, kidnappings, or robberies take place at these locations mainly because you are stationary. Something as simple as not only getting your gas from a certain location, but also when you get gas. Daytime is best. Especially if you are a woman. Another sometimes overlooked place is a person's home. Who doesn't feel safe in their own home? This is when a lot of people get relaxed and let their guards down. How hard is it for someone to conceal themselves behind a tree or in some bushes and wait for you to come out or pull up?

The point is, like we started this card off, there are countless dangers that lurk behind every corner. Again, stay security minded at all times. Don't be overly comfortable anywhere at any time, around anyone. You create opportunities for others to harm you by being lax. Don't be. Make it hard, if not outright impossible, for others to get at you. Anyone that comes in your presence must be mentally shook down. Closeness equates to danger. The more remote someone is from you, generally you are safer.

* Key Points:
    a. Potential harm exists everywhere
    b. Practice general security measures
    c. Master evasive maneuvers
    d. Don't become predictable
    e. Always think safety first
    f. Comfortability is dangerous

Card 9: The Great Falling Away

Great - Remarkable in magnitude, degree, or effectiveness.

Fall - The act of falling by the force of gravity. A falling out, off, or away from.

Away - Out of existence. Gone.

* Concept/Objective: Some things must happen in order for other things to happen. In order for you to be what you want to be, you must rid yourself of certain things. Great changes need to take place with you before you are able to reach and maintain a certain level of greatness.

(Questions)

1. Why must some things happen before other things can happen?
2. What things must you rid yourself of in order to

be more than what you have been?
3. How are masterpieces produced?

"Let no man deceive you by any means: for THAT DAY shall not come, except there come A FALLING AWAY FIRST...". 10

What day? The day when your true greatness will emerge forth from you. The day when you are able to control circumstances rather than them controlling you. The day when you are able to do as you please no matter who or what. The day when all your cares will be swept away. That day will never come unless and until there is a falling away first of those things that keep the real you buried. There is an entire reality, a whole world right inside you that needs to be unwrapped. You are so much more than sometimes you may think you are, and you can do way more than what you may think you are capable of doing.

Just think about something you desire to do. No matter what it is. Someplace you desire to go. No matter where it is. Someone you desire to be. No matter who it is. Now think about the things that are preventing you from doing that thing, going to that place, or being that person. It is these things that must be eradicated from you, and destroyed until you wipe them completely out of existence. The opposite is true when it comes to things you need to add to yourself. When this happens, you will be on the dawn of a new horizon.

In both small and great ways, it is a matter of what are you willing to put yourself through to be able to do anything you put your mind to, to go any place you desire to go, or to become the person you always wanted to be and knew you could be. What are you willing to give up? What are you willing to stop doing? Can you divest yourself of trivial pursuits, bad habits, or unproductive tendencies that are blockages to you bringing forth your greatness or achieving long sought after goals or aspirations?

When you give those things up, you are not losing anything, you are only replacing them with something better for something greater. But in order to do this it takes an exceptional ability to sacrifice things you may hold dear and discipline yourself to standards you think are superhuman. Do you think you have what it takes? Can you willfully stop engaging in self-destructive activities? Can you sacrifice engaging in temporal pleasures? Can you disassociate yourself from people who don't want for themselves what you want for yourself?

When you can answer yes to these questions, then good for you, if not, then woe. You should only consider these previously asked questions if there is an element of dissatisfaction in you that makes you desirous of something different, something better, and something more real and tangible in your life. It goes without saying that if you are content with where you are in life then you will continue as you are. It is entirely up to you to decide what you want for yourself. If your stance is one where you want to be a better version of yourself, then there are qualifying factors that must be a part of your formula for producing such results.

How can you get to the point where you are able to exercise mastery or control over situations and circumstances in life, if you are unable to exercise this same mastery or control over yourself? This is what is meant by some things must happen in order for other things to happen. This is the natural order of things. Everything begins with you. It all starts within. Any condition you find yourself in is only reflective, to some degree or another, of your internal state. You may think this is a tall order, and it is, but it is one you are well equipped to fill.

This is why nothing is more beneficial than developing an iron clad will that will give you the necessary strength to sculpt yourself into a master. And nothing is more harmful than giving in to weaknesses that further weakens your internal fortitude which sabotages any efforts you've made up to any given point. So, what are some of the things you need to carve completely out of your life?

Well, you know that better than anyone else. This can be any number of things; from laziness to being socially inept, from drug abuse or other types of intoxicants to not being studious enough and feeding your mind inferior things via low conversations or television, from being sexually unrestrained to hanging around unproductive people or places, etc.

Now you know the secret to how masterpieces are produced. By chiseling away from yourself anything that is not art. Once this is done, what will you have left other than what you envisioned in your mind? A masterpiece. A work of art. This is what you are, the most exquisite creature under the sun. It's just somewhere along the way so much crap has covered you and so much crap has been put in you. Let it all fall away and your greatness will shine forth.

* **Key Points:**
    a. You will never be more today by continuing to do the same old thing you did yesterday
    b. There is an entire reality, a whole world right inside you that needs to be unwrapped
    c. You have the power to do what you desire, go where you want, and be who you choose to be
    d. Mastery of self precedes mastery of anything else
    e. Divest yourself of trivial pursuits, bad habits, and unproductive tendencies
    f. Masterpieces are produced by chiseling away from you anything that is not art

Card 10: Sheer Determination

Sheer - Being free from an adulterant. Pure, Unmixed.

Determination - The act of deciding definitely and firmly. A firm or fixed intention to achieve a desired end.

* Concept/Objective: Develop a mindset of accomplishing what you set out to accomplish irrespective of what you are up against. Never be deterred by setbacks or disappointments. Developing a resolve to persevere despite whatever or whoever, is something that has to come from deep within yourself.

(Questions)
1. How do you persevere despite overwhelming odds?
2. What is the formula for developing the right state of mind needed to never quit or give up?
3. Why is being determined the determining factor as to whether you reach your goals or not?

There is a certain tenaciousness of spirit that is required to achieve exceptional goals and it also requires a tremendous amount of sacrifice. Consistency and intensity of effort will inevitably bring you closer and closer to reaching your goals. The closer you get to your goals, things begin to come up that can make you question yourself and your ability to finish what you set out to do. What are they?

You will be tested from within and without. Your strength and will begin to diminish. You begin to run on reserves when it comes to patience, energy, desire, and so on. You get exhausted. You begin to feel overwhelmed by the forces that you are up against. It is only when you get closer to accomplishing something, anything, that you just have to dig your heels in. Go within yourself and pull something up out of you that you didn't even know existed. Something that will give you your proverbial second wind.

It all starts in your mind and how you think. Your mental disposition is the key to unlocking your inner power reserve that we all have. Overwhelming odds can actually work in your favor. Have you ever wondered why some people perform better under pressure? They perform better when they have to, when their back is against the wall. This is the same thing with perseverance. Your condition has put you in a tight spot. One where it demands of you a mighty response to change that condition. One of perseverance and determination.

You persevere by persevering. You persevere because you are determined. You persevere because you have to. I mean what else is there? What other choice do you have? You persevere because the alternative is not an option and is unacceptable. You develop tunnel vision where all you see is the end result. And in your mind, come hell or high water, nothing or no one is going to stop you.

The formula to get you in this mindset is: Total Dissatisfaction + Unwavering Desire + Strong Will = Right State of Mind

You have to ask yourself, how dissatisfied am I with my present condition? What kind of desire do I have to fuel me in getting out of this condition? Is my will strong enough to carry me through the many obstacles that are before me? When you can say to yourself that you are completely dissatisfied, that your desire is not fleeting from one goal to the next, and you have an indomitable will, then you know you have the winning formula for success.

Once you determine in your mind that you will do a thing, no matter what it is, no matter how long it takes, and no matter the opposition, then it is as good as done. Being determined means that your mind is made up, and nothing can defeat a made up mind. You have a no quit, no surrender attitude. If you don't possess this mindset, then you can become easily dissuaded.

Things will always come up that can interfere with you reaching your goals. Depending upon whatever it is, you either have to ignore it or deal with it. Ignoring something means that it will go away on its own, so you don't give it the time of day. The things that won't simply go away on their own have to be dealt with in such a way that it both; removes it from your path, and it does not take you off course.

Having a singular focus is important. You can't be all over the place. When your time, your thoughts, or your energies, are spread over many areas or are in many different places at the same time, then you decrease significantly the success of any one of those tasks. It is better to concentrate on one thing at a time than a multiplicity of things.

If you place a 1,000 lb. weight over an area of 10 sq. feet, with the weight being evenly distributed, and take that same 1,000 lb. weight being evenly distributed over an area of 1 sq. foot; how much force or pressure would be exerted per sq. inch on the 10 sq. foot area as opposed to the 1 sq. foot area? The smaller the surface or area equates to more pound for pound pressure being exerted.

The same is true of spreading yourself out over many things. You greatly diminish the effect that can be had in any one area because your point of impact is less than what it could be if all your energy was directed at one point. The bottom line is this; having too many irons in the fire is not good.

Lastly, on the matter of unreached goals; it takes an exceptionally great person to stick with it in the face of many different adversities. Yes, fatigue can set in, but you have to find a way to resist giving in to it. How many times has someone given up on something when they were right on the precipice of reaching their goal? Too many to probably number.

The point is, no matter how much you feel inclined to, don't stop. Keep going. People need a reason to do what they do. A motive. Find a reason to keep going. Without that, you lose the incentive to weather the storms that are a natural part of the process of reaching goals or being successful.

* Key Points:
- a. Consistency and intensity of effort are important keys to reaching your goals
- b. The greater the pressure you are up against, the more determined you should be
- c. Develop the right state of mind
- d. Allow overwhelming odds to work in your favor
- e. Focus on one main thing at a time
- f. Find a reason to keep going

Card 11: Thicker and Blacker

Thick - Impenetrable; Unconcerned; Profound.

Black - Effective action without regard to how the consequences will affect others. Ruthless, but not necessarily evil.

* Concept/Objective: No matter how bold, shrewd, or ruthless someone is, you must be bolder, shrewder, and more ruthless. You are supreme. And you must dominate supremely. Never take the lesser position. Be thicker and blacker than those around you and you will excel beyond measure.

(Questions)
1. What is meant by thicker and blacker and how can you become such?
2. Can you please explain the concept of detachment and its role in your pursuit of power?
3. Why is learning how to strategically yield so powerful?

"When you conceal your will from others, that is thick; When you force your will on others, that is black." 5

Thick Face, Black Heart, as a concept, began in 1911 as a theory under the title, Thick Black Theory. Because of the uproar surrounding the first of a three-part scheduled release, the other two parts were not published, until some time later. The original writing was barely 2000 words long. After undergoing several revisions and partial banment, yet it thrives.

I think it is necessary at the outset to properly set the stage for what the reader will encounter while reading this card. This card perhaps will be the one which has the greatest potential to be misunderstood. At the same, it is this card that is the crux of all the others. It focuses exclusively on the ability to achieve great results utilizing the most ruthless tactics. How you read this is dependent on how you understand and apply the term 'ruthlessness'.

Aside from its negative connotation, ruthlessness is merely the basis of effective action. This action is not necessarily evil. Although it can be. Yet, it will challenge your view of good and evil and stretch your understanding of it to its limits. There are many examples to draw from to prove this point. However, I am not concerned with that at this juncture. You will have to draw those parallels on your own. Remember in the introduction to this book we said that power is not always pretty, nor is it always expressed the same way. The entire concept of Thick Face, Black Heart is a perfect example of that.

Thick Face, Black Heart, is a concept that on the outside shows no signs of being bothered by others' perceptions of you, while at the same time having an inner strength and ability to execute efficiently with a certain kind of ruthlessness. The former, Thick Face, is concerned with basically developing thick skin. Breaking away from the norm of worrying about how you look in the eyes of others while pursuing your goals. The latter, Black Heart, is concerned with your overall ability to act in the most appropriate manner for the occasion, as long as you benefit. The dual aspect of achieving this is from a single concept but expressed by various means according to your own development and the conditions you are faced with. There are three phases to this whole process which are:

Phase One: Winning At All Costs

The first stage: thick as a castle wall, black as charcoal. This is the level of the cheap hustler, crook, and con man. Although the face is as thick as a castle wall, it is penetrable. Their blackness is apparent to all who see them. They are distasteful and repulsive in everyone's eyes.

The second stage: thick and hard, black and shimmering. These are the more advanced practitioners. They have strengthened their face by hardening it; they have polished their Black Heart by making it more appealing. They are no longer the cheap hustler. Their outward appearance is respectable...

The third stage: so thick it is formless, so black it is colorless—the highest level...". 5

Phase Two: Self-Inquiry

Beneath Phase One lie deeper essences of Thick Face, Black Heart, they find it to be repellent, even to themselves. Consequently, they begin a process of self-inquiry. Self-inquiry is a spiritual process. We cannot honestly address Thick Face, Black Heart without mentioning the spiritual side of life...Those who practice Thick Face, Black Heart without the cultivation of Phase Two can become dangerous people. At this stage of self-inquiry, the individual is often vulnerable because he has rejected the powerful, wicked behaviors of Phase

One...at this stage he may look disheveled and be considered disjointed by others, within himself he is going through a powerful transformation." 5

Phase Three: The Warrior

This final phase is the combination of both previous phases. Here you will be able to create a meeting ground for the sublime and the ruthless... After Phase Two the practitioner becomes indifferent and courageous. He adopts the warrior's attitude—dispassion and detachment. He sees life as a battle that must be fought. There is no way out. Victory is the only aim. He dispassionately does battle with the wicked outer elements while courageously facing his inner enemies. He is then able to detach from them, so that their presence does not thwart him. This is the power of detachment and dispassion that enables the warrior to face life's challenges with calm and grace."   5

All of us are, in one way or another, a practitioner of Thick Face, Black Heart. Maybe not on a level, or in a way that the most experienced are, but we are. Our perception of how we should view things, especially ourselves, and how we should act, especially in regards to others, has been ingrained in us all our lives. We live our lives according to this internal belief system and it affects every part of our lives, all of our lives. The more boxed in our thinking is, based upon whatever it is we believe in, the less effective we will be in our actions. This is part of the reason why we are in the condition we are in. This is also the reason why we will remain in such condition. And it will never change until we become a better, more advanced practitioner of Thick Face, Black Heart.

The ability to detach yourself and become dispassionate towards someone or something takes a certain kind of mind. Not everyone can easily do this. Your own sense of morality and conscience can sometimes get in the way. There will be tough decisions to be made that may conflict with your sense of right and wrong or good and evil. This internal conflict, depending upon which side wins, will determine if you win. You are advised against making emotionally based decisions not rooted in logic.

Good businessmen have to make tough decisions at times so that their businesses can survive during turbulent times. From the outside, depending on what types of cost effective decisions they have to make, they could be viewed as ruthless and callous. If these businessmen did not have a thick enough face to make black hearted decisions, their businesses would go under. They are forced to be thick faced and black hearted for   survival's sake. You too must be the same. Become detached and your decisions will produce greater and more effective results.

Strategic yielding is so important in practicing

Thick Face, Black Heart because it is a premiere defensive posture. One that allows you to bide time, calculate, and confuse your opponents. Consider the following;

"In order to protect yourself as you practice Thick Face, Black Heart, first acquire the power of yielding. Your outward action may seem to be submissive and nonthreatening, but inwardly, never lose sight of your objectives. When you can win a battle by maneuvering obliquely, why go for a frontal assault? When your opponent perceives you as no threat, he may not be moved to pull out his biggest guns when dealing with you. But if you forewarn him and overexaggerate your strength, he will be obligated to use his most effective weapons on you." 5

No matter how thick someone is, you must be thicker. No matter how black someone is, you must be blacker. If someone is tactful, subtle, detached, dangerous, good, subversive, or are able to remain unaffected, then you must be all of that too, but to a more superlative degree. Sooner or later, all of these abilities will be put to the test. This pocket of power, should you choose to enter it, will undoubtedly change your life for the better. Seek to learn and understand Thick Face, Black Heart principles because proper understanding precedes proper action. I will end this card with the following quote and comment;

"The natural way of Thick Face, Black Heart is beyond human manipulation, beyond the petty standards of human judgment. When one acts in harmony with the Universal Will, one's actions are aligned with the good of all and the benefit of all. You are neither self-righteous nor too eager to please; nor are you seeking approval. In action, you are swift, competent, and dispassionate. In yielding, you are unabashed and have no concern for others' judgments. In conquering, you are effective and can be ruthless. In action and non-action, you are changeless. You are a true Thick Face, Black Heart practitioner." 5

All in all, nothing here should be taken as a license to do whatever you want, to whoever you want, however you want. Not all in all. You have the right to do so, as with anything you do. Yet, there are Universal Principles to contend with. You are being introduced to a methodology, which when perfected and practiced, will give you a decided advantage against anyone.

There exists many at every level of society who have no moral overtones and are the crudest when it comes to winning at all costs. From the highest echelons of government and business to the average person. Those who have no conscience are the most detached of all and are the most dangerous of all. If nothing else, be very aware of its usage against you and protect yourself from being victimized by those whose face is so thick it is formless, and so black it is colorless.

* Key Points:
   a. Aside from its negative connotation, ruthlessness is merely the basis for effective action
   b. Being Thick Faced is developing thick skin so as not to be moved by the opinions and judgments of others
   c. Having a Black Heart is becoming so concerned with nothing but the end result even if you have to be ruthless
   d. Winning at all costs, self-inquiry, and the warrior, are the three phases of Thick Face, Black Heart
   e. Your condition will remain unchanged unless you become a better, more advanced practitioner of Thick Face, Black Heart
   f. You are advised against making emotionally based decisions not rooted in logic
   g. Learn how to yield when and where necessary to position yourself for a strategic win

Card 12: Personal Grooming Habits

Personal - Of, relating to, or affecting a particular person. Private. Individual.

Groom - To get into readiness for a specific objective.

Habit - A behavior pattern acquired by frequent repetition. Something done so regularly that it becomes almost an involuntary and instinctive act.

* *Concept/Objective: By engaging regularly in acts that will cultivate your real power, which is internal and unseen, you will be poised at every turn to create opportunities for yourself and to take advantage of unexpected ones. You will no longer be at the mercy of others. As your power increases you will be able to accomplish your goals in less time and with greater ease.*

(Questions)
1. When it comes to grooming, what do you think is one of the greatest inventions ever made, and why?
2. How often should you concern yourself with grooming?
3. What happens when power does not justify itself at every turn?

"The practice of a cultivated man is to refine himself by quietude and develop virtue by frugality. Without detachment, there is no way to clarify the will, without serenity, there is no way to get far. Study requires calm, talent requires study. Without study there is no way to expand talent; without calm there is no way to accomplish study.".[1]

The mirror, by far, is one of the greatest inventions ever made when it comes to grooming. Before mirrors, one had to find any reflective surface to see themselves in or rely on someone else's help to see what they themselves could not see. Mirrors allow you to see yourself so that you can groom more effectively. When you notice something that is out of place, even a single hair, you fix it. If you see something on your face that shouldn't be there, you remove it. Without a good mirror, one cannot groom in the best manner possible. No reflective surface, or the helpful eyes of any other person can substitute for a good mirror. No one can see you better than you, and no one can make the necessary corrections you need to make better than you.

You should know by now that we are not talking about any ordinary mirror. We are not talking about any ordinary grooming. We are talking about the mirror of introspection where you look at and inspect yourself from the inside out. Introspection allows you to look deep within yourself to discover all that needs to be developed. You are being guided with this card to focus on and cultivate the best part of yourself, which is your mind, and its constant need to be groomed.

In order to get back what you lost you must become fully engaged in the process to restore what has been lost and stolen. I read a book some time ago which had a very powerful title, which was, 'They stole it but you must return it.' No matter how you were deprived of the power of your mind, whether through systematic means or self-destructive ones, it is up to you to get it back. This responsibility is exclusively yours and no one else's. If you call yourself waiting for someone else to do for you what you can do for yourself, then you will continue to suffer as a result and the blame will be all yours.

Grooming is a regular practice, a daily process, and it is one that should become so habitual at that you begin to instinctively make this internal grooming a part of your everyday regimen. In fact, there should be no occasion where you are not found grooming your power. Every day you should hone your skills. Every day you should be learning something. Every day you should be getting better at something. Every day you should be making improvements. Do this and you will be immaculately groomed.

Grooming is a very personal and private matter, it takes place in a private setting. But the effects of it are seen publicly. When you study, do it privately. Don't broadcast it. When you fast, no one should be the wiser. When you meditate, find a quiet, isolated, and secluded place, even if it is in a room full of people, be as if you were alone. Your power will grow and grow. The power of your mind will radiate power. You won't be able to conceal it even if you tried to. The only time you should actively display your power is when it is necessary to do so and it will serve a needed purpose. Otherwise, never parade your power, it is uncivil to do so. Although people respect and fear power, which is expected and needed, but they will despise you if you brandish it indiscriminately.

Stability and power are not synonymous. There is a lot of flux in the realm of power. Things constantly change. One minute you are at the top, the next you can find yourself in a free fall. To prevent this, power must always justify itself. If not, its stance will fall immediately. There are certain methodologies and practices that are attributable to garnering power, maintaining it, and furthering it. The same thing that made you rise, if not continued, will be the means of your demise.

Don't ever get too comfortable with your power once you start growing into it or allow it to cause you to have an exaggerated view of yourself or others. Always use the best of what is available to groom yourself. When you do this, you are assured the best results. Develop good habits that enhance your power. Destroy bad ones that inhibit it. All knowledge is interrelated in some way, so when you are striving for mastery in any art, it requires knowledge of several arts.

"Man can have nothing but what he strives for, and that his striving will soon be seen." [11]

* Key Points:

a. The mirror, by far, is one of the greatest inventions ever made when it comes to grooming yourself
b. You must become fully engaged to get back what has been lost and stolen
c. There should be no occasion where you are not found grooming your power
d. Grooming is a very personal and private matter, it takes place in a private setting
e. Power must always justify itself, or its stance will fall immediately
f. Develop good habits that enhance your power. Destroy bad ones that inhibit it

Card 13: Atmospheric Conditions

Atmosphere - A surrounding influence or environment.

Condition - A state of being.

* Concept/Objective: Learn how to control your atmosphere. Your influential ability depends on it. Air has many properties to it. It can either be good to breathe or not. Concern yourself with becoming a breath of fresh air. Create an atmosphere around yourself that everyone wants to be around.

(Questions)

1. Why should it be important to you about what you give off to others?

2. What is an ideal atmospheric condition and how can you produce it?
3. How can you protect yourself from certain hostile environments?

The essence of atmospheric conditions is rooted in the core of your thinking. Your thoughts, the more recurrent they are, no matter what kind they are, emit a certain energy, and this energy produces an aura around you, an atmosphere if you will. No matter what you think about, it can be felt by others. When anyone comes in your presence, the atmosphere you created for yourself will affect others in one way or another. And depending upon how you affect others when they come around you, this will dictate to a large degree how you and that other person's relationship will be.

Our goal is to garner more control over our lives and the various situations we will inevitably find ourselves in. Remember, none of us are as powerless as perhaps we have been. Why relinquish control over any situation if we don't have to? Don't forget, the devil is in the details. This will be repeated again from another context somewhere in the next section because of its importance and because the things that you may think are insignificant are greater than you think.

Just look at the small mustard seed in comparison to what it can produce and you will see how something so small has the potential to balloon into something much greater. When we exercise control over matters early on, things can be prevented or at minimum turn out differently. We should never take a "it doesn't matter" approach. Everything matters and everything is connected with other things even though it may seem as if it doesn't. Many fail to comprehend the interconnectedness of things.

This connection can be direct or indirect; it can take shape in the present or in the future, whatever the case, unless you are mindful of this then you will always be perplexed why things seem to turn out a certain way in your life. You simply wander through life being oblivious to and not concerned with things that you should take a little more seriously.

All I am saying here is that there are widespread implications when we don't recognize and follow universal principles that are always present and they govern every situation. Laws govern everything whether they are written or unwritten or known or unknown. And the more you are conscious of these laws and how they should be recognized and followed, the more in control of your life you will be.

The laws of thought are no different. How you think is important if you want to produce a specific atmosphere around yourself. Let us make a comparison of two different atmospheric conditions. One is a sunny 70° day, low to no humidity, and a slight fifteen-mile-per-hour breeze; the other one is -30°, with a wind chill of -45°, and blizzard conditions.

Generally speaking, if someone had a choice to choose between the two, which atmospheric condition do you think most people would want to be in? And why? Which one would almost every want nothing to do with? And why? Most everyone would want to be out and about enjoying that 70° weather. This would not be the case in extremely frigid conditions. Hardly anyone would want to be in that kind of weather. There really is no comparison for obvious reasons.

Did you know, or do you believe that how you think can either produce the 70° day or the -30° day? You have the power and the ability to create an atmosphere around you where everyone wants to be around you and be in your presence, or you can be reflective of that condition that hardly anyone would want to be in.

Suppose someone, no matter when you are in their presence, is always warm, vibrant, positive and encouraging. As opposed to someone who is always cold, a chronic complainer, negative, and disparaging. One would be welcomed and draw us in, while the other would repel us and keep us away. This is the power of atmospheric conditions.

The vibe we get from others, or the energy they

emit, informs us of their predominant thoughts. These are the type of people to be avoided. Most of us do this naturally, but there are times when we may ignore this type of person. Just know that positivity begets positivity and negativity begets negativity. Each of these bring different things in their wake.

One last point on atmospheric conditions. Some conditions can be so hostile that they can have a dilapidating effect on us that they change us for the worse. The best remedy for this is for you to become so developed by grooming your power as discussed in the last card so that your environment will be affected by you no matter how hostile it is and not you by it. I want to show you an example of what can happen when you do or don't equip yourself in this way by giving you a picture using something I came across many years ago that I think will get the point over better.

Picture in your mind a raw carrot, an uncooked shelled egg, and a few ounces of coffee grounds. All three of these are placed into a separate pot of boiling water, which is symbolic of an hostile environment. Notice the characteristics of each prior to entering the boiling water, or hostile environment. Place each in its own pot for a while. Then afterwards, examine the characteristics of each and note the specific changes each underwent.

The carrot, prior to being placed in the pot of

boiling water was strong and firm, but after being in that hostile environment for a while it became soft, weak, infirm, and pliable

Take the uncooked shelled egg now. Its characteristics are that it has a soft inside with a natural hard protective covering. After being in the boiling water it undergoes certain changes too. Its insides now begin to harden.

The coffee grounds are separated and scattered before being in the boiling water. Their environment caused them to come together, or you could say forced them to. However, the difference between the carrot, the egg, and the coffee is that the carrot and egg were affected by their environment, while the coffee greatly affected its environment.

The environment, or boiling pot of hot water that the ground coffee was placed in was not the same anymore, it reflected and was colored by the coffee grounds. The change that it did do to the coffee grounds is that it forced them to come together to combat the hostility of its environment. The first two changes, that of the carrot and the egg, were for the worse, while the third was for the better notwithstanding it darkened things up. Think over that.

Hostile environments can either make you or break you. These types of atmospheric conditions do not have to negatively affect you, but they can. You can go into a situation strong and firm, like the raw carrot, and be affected so much that it can strip you of your strength and weaken you. You can become weak and feeble. You could also be adversely affected like the uncooked shelled egg, going into a hostile environment with a lot of love for humanity, resembling the soft interior of the egg, then you can be turned from that into a hard and callous human being with no concern at all for anything or anyone.

The choice is yours. You can either reflect the carrot, the egg, or the coffee. Either way, the point is that atmospheric conditions are important. The ones we produce, the ones others produce, and how they can affect you or you it.

In the end, there is a dual aspect to this.

* **Key Points:**
    a. The essence of atmospheric conditions is rooted in the core of your thinking
    b. You are not powerless over your atmosphere and how you can affect others
    c. Things that are in seed form has the potential to balloon into something much greater
    d. Don't ignore universal principles and their widespread implications when it comes to being mindful of what we give off to others
    e. Let the vibe or energy of others determine if or how you deal with them
    f. Affect your environment and don't be affected by it

SECTION TWO

♥

HEARTS

* Commentary II:

Imagine being a soldier, out on the battlefield, in the middle of war, without any teaching or training; that is a very grim, extremely dangerous, and even deadly situation to be in. The same could be said about life. To give people life without teaching them how to live it is called abandoning them. Most of us learn about life unconventionally. This way of learning, which is primarily by way of experience, has caused much pain and hardship that could have been avoided had we learned by more conventional means. But because many of us haven't, we too are in a very grim, extremely dangerous and even deadly situation similar to that of the untaught and untrained soldier.

There is a segment in society that fits this mold and continues to be deprived of the main essentials of life that will allow them to survive, let alone flourish. This group has loss all hope of a better condition. Hope is the last line of defense for the realization of a way out. When all hope is gone, there is nothing to look forward to. Only death waits. And if all you see is death in front of you, then how do you expect a person like this to live their life?

Fret not, you have in your possession a vehicle by which you can arm yourself with what you need to win, irrespective of the score. Coming back from a large deficit takes more of everything from you and in you than it does to keep an already large lead.

The advantage you have is that the odds of you winning is slim to none. And this is how those in front of you think. In doing so, they have a tendency of letting up as they cruise to what they think is an easy victory. While they are doing this, you are gaining more and more ground, and before anyone is the wiser, you have not only caught up, but you have surpassed those previously ahead of you.

Each of these cards are designed to provide you with the tools to exercise a greater degree of control and mastery over the various situations and circumstances you will be in. In a very real sense you are being weaponized. Your mind is the best weapon you have. And as you develop it, you become that much more potent. You will become a force to be reckoned with. As you mentally consume something more substantive than what you have been taking in, your thoughts will begin to elevate beyond where they were, and this is when you will be able to take more control over your life.

Now that you have been through the first section, you are more ready to embrace that which will follow. You were warned in the introduction that you would be exposed to a unique perspective. Have you? It was also suggested to you that you have to take what you read and make it your own. This means that you should personalize to whatever degree you desire, the principles of power you are being acquainted with as they fit into your life or a particular situation. There is never a cookie cutter approach to all things. You have to tailor whatever you do to fit the occasion. Grab hold of what is good for you and discard the rest.

What you won't be able to do upon the completion of each section is to use the excuse that you didn't know. That you are ill equipped. That you are without the knowledge of the landscape of power and its many dynamics. The onus is now on you. Do with it what you will.

(Power Poses)

Cards 14 - 26:

14. Chameleonistic Stances; 15. Money Matters; 16. The Irrevocable Power of Thought; 17. Adversarial Companionship; 18. Preparing for all Eventualities; 19. Insultive Indulgences; 20. The Royal Crown Affair; 21. The Undeniable Power of Magnetism; 22. Team Building; 23. Interrogatories; 24. The Talking Skull; 25. Minimizing Mistakes; 26. Total Domination

Card 14: Chameleonistic Stances

Chameleon - A lizard with an unusual ability to change colors to blend in with their environment so they can go undetected, chiefly as a defense mechanism against predators. One who is subject to quick changes, esp. as it relates to their appearance.

Stance - A way of standing, being placed, or positioning oneself.

* Concept/Objective: Sticking out like a sore thumb is a sure way to expose you in ways that are not good. Blend in to your environment. Become one with it by emulation. You be like a fly on a wall, no one will be aware of your presence unless you make a move. Master the art of camouflage and you can be anyone and go anywhere.

(Questions)
1. What makes emulating a chameleon a premiere pose?
2. At what point is unmasking oneself a more preferable and necessary stance?
3. Why and how are false flag missions deceptively powerful?

"I am made all things to all men..." 10

Although there are animals that are more adept at adapting to their environment by masterfully mirroring their surroundings, the chameleon has been nominated as the emblem of such ability. The principle is simple, blend in. The more unnoticeable you are, the safer you are, the more in control you can be, and the more room you will have to maneuver. By assuming this posture you have all the leverage and tactical advantages for a wide array of maneuvers.

If you are naturally a colorful person and you like to peacock, then it will take more effort on your behalf to quell your colors. And it will serve you well to do so. This is not the arena for flamboyancy. To become chameleonistic is to become a tactical genius. When you are able to become one with your environment, at will, then you have mastered the ability to play with appearances. Don't underestimate the power contained in this stance.

The range you may have to adapt to is broad and varied. Being able to do this physically is only one dimension. You also have mental, moral, and spiritual dimensions to master as well. You should never have a problem with pretending. If you do, then you won't be successful in practicing this art. Actors do it all the time. They understand it is only a role they are playing. And that role more often than not does not reflect any part of them in their real everyday life. Once that role is over, they resume their regularly scheduled selves.

"Outwardly, be gracious. Adapt to their every mood. Enter their spirit. Inwardly, calculate and wait: your surrender is a strategy not a way of life.

When the time comes, and it inevitably will, the tables will turn." 3

You can win more by blending in than by sticking out. Openness is appropriate only when it is appropriate. All other occasions require a sort of creativity and ingenuity when both trying to infiltrate by blending in and as a cover from being noticed or exposed. Utilize whatever is necessary to maximize your advantage in any given situation. The flexibility this move gives you makes it a premiere pose.

There will be times when your authentic self needs to surface from the deep by removing your mask. Any move that you ever make is guided by what will work best to get the intended result. So if uncovering yourself will work better, then so be it. Your instinctual sensitiveness will be so heightened that it will inform you in the most subtle way in the direction you should go.

In instances where someone is attempting to emulate the chameleon as you are, and you know that to be the case, allow them to continue on. By speaking up or calling them out, guess what, you have given your position up and you expose yourself. The object is for you to be aware of their presence, not the other way around. Unless of course it is to your advantage to do so.

Everything in nature has a natural defense system. Human beings are no different. However, humans' adaptableness makes them more able to infiltrate or deceive more so than any other creature. False flag missions are so deceptively powerful because they are designed to allow someone to gain access to an area that they would generally be closed off from.

When you garb yourself in your enemies clothing, in their mannerisms, or their culturistic practices, defenses are lowered and access is granted. Had you come in your own clothing, in your own mannerisms, or your own culture, then you would have stood out, and thereby would have been denied entrance in that circle or group.

Learning as much as you can about other peoples will enable you to make yourself up to resemble that group. Sort of like a professional makeup artist. This entails learning the language and the walk. So much so that you become indistinguishable from the native of that group or people because of your disguise. When you can become a master of disguises, your false flag missions will prove to be unstoppable. For the most effective false flag missions there is no known defense.

In the animal world, blending in serves a dual purpose, one if you are a predator, another if you are the prey. If blending in fails, the stakes are higher for the latter. While a predator may lose a meal, the prey will lose its life. The stakes may not be this high in the human world, but the principles are just the same. There will always be something to be both gained and loss depending upon the effectiveness of your ability to blend it. Camouflage is another term that is also befitting to describe what we have been discussing all along.

*** Key Points:**
    a. The main objective of assuming a chameleonistic stance is to be able to blend in
    b. There is no peacocking or flamboyancy allowed in the arena of concealment
    c. To become a master in this art you must learn how to play with appearances
    d. Openness is only appropriate when it is appropriate
    e. To gain access to generally closed off areas, employ the false flag principle
    f. When you become a master of disguises, your false flag missions will prove to be unstoppable

Card 15: Money Matters

Money - Something generally accepted as a medium of exchange. Currency.

Matter - A subject under consideration.

* Concept/Objective: Money is at the center of much activity. It is the primal means of getting things accomplished. Money equals freedom. Not having it is not an option. Money is not a sin, but not having it is.

The Master's Deck

(Questions)
1. How is power a form of currency?
2. Why is money considered, in some schools of thought, the root of all evil? And in others, the answer to all things?
3. When it is all said and done, what should your attitude be about money?

Money makers are the real movers and shakers in a world where everything has a price, and almost anyone can be bought. The amount of money that the very rich has and makes is staggering. The power they wield as a result is even more staggering. In addition to money, power became their currency. Picture this:

It was reported, "John D. Rockefeller sleeps eight and one-half hours every night, retiring at 10:30 and rising at 7. Every morning when he gets up he is $17,705 richer than he was when he went to bed. He sits down to breakfast at 8 o'clock and leaves the table at 8:30, and in that short half hour his wealth has grown $1,041.50. On Sunday he goes to church, and in the two hours he is away from home his riches have grown $4,166. His nightly amusements is playing the violin. Every evening when he picks up the instrument he is $50,000 richer than he was when he laid it down the previous night." 9

This turns the phrase, 'making money while you

sleep' on its head. And this made Rockefeller America's first ever billionaire. To Rockefeller, competition was a sin. He ruthlessly destroyed any would-be competitors. It was all about monopolization. There are only two sinful things about money; one is not having it, the other is 'competition'.

Money has no intrinsic value or moralistic qualities. Yet, it has the power to bring out the best and the worst in man. Whenever money is involved, a host of other things are added as well. What some will do for money is limitless and almost unimaginable. Making money is all that matters. Whoever has to be lied to, scammed, or crossed out makes no difference. Money does not have to be the root of all evil, as some would say, but it does have the power to turn you into something that is frightening.

In this world, money is king, it is God, and it rules profoundly. He who has the money wears the crown. Money is power. With money and power, problems are easily solved and done away with. They both can be used to get you what you want. Making both of them, money and power, a form of currency. They say more money, more problems. But rich people problems and poor people problems are not one and the same. Which problems would you rather have?

A fool and his money will soon depart because he is unwise when it comes to money matters. Become knowledgeable of money and its many secrets. One of its biggest secrets is debt. Debt is a tool used to enslave people. Ordinary people don't understand debt the way they should. If they did, they would steer clear of it. Questionable financial decisions can compound a person's debt way out of proportion. Debt keeps people impoverished. This is just one of the many pitfalls of money. The poor stay poor because they make poor decisions.

Poverty is a crime against humanity. Nothing is more violent, more devastating, or more dangerous than poverty. The residual effect of poverty is beyond measure. When a person is deprived of what is called a livable wage, and is cut off from many viable means of making a decent living, it engenders all sorts of extreme acts for its accrual. You are first penalized for being poor, then again for engaging in whatever manner you deem necessary to come up out of poverty. This is the epitome of a lose-lose situation.

Your attitude about money should be that it is indispensable and a vital necessity in getting things accomplished. Once you learn the secret of money, and its unique language, you will profit from everything and everyone, by making money always in all ways. How you do this is limited only by your imagination. Little do people know that, 'Behind every great fortune is a crime.'   9

Study the histories of the historically rich and how they made their massive fortunes. Every one of them, at their very root, is some form of criminal activity. What drove them was their insatiable appetite for money and power. This is not a license for you to scheme, embezzle, or defraud anyone like they did. Just stating facts.

This card would be incomplete without making mention of the most powerful secretive banking dynasty ever, the Rothschild's, who were master money manipulators. Their web was so far-reaching that it spanned centuries and continents. The most prominent American businessmen of that era owe their vast fortunes to the Rothschilds who financed them.

They, the Rothschilds, had a hand in financing every significant industry from oil (John D. Rockefeller), steel (Andrew Carnegie), railroads (Edward Harriman), and of course banking (John P. Morgan). He who controls the money, holds all the power. This is the lesson that you must learn and cling to.

Become business minded. Develop an attitude where you are always sniffing out opportunities to explore various business ventures. From real estate to the stock market. From franchises to clothing. From media to any number of small businesses. From clubs to non- or for-profits. Nothing is off limits if it will generate money. Just be smart and do your due diligence. And above all, and this is so important, learn to network.

* **Key Points:**
    a. Power itself is a form of currency
    b. Money has no intrinsic value or moral quality
    c. He who has the money wears the crown
    d. Money talks and is a language all its own, one that you should become fluent in
    e. Poverty is a crime against humanity
    f. Make money always in all ways
    g. Networking is important

Card 16: The Irrevocable Power of Thought

Irrevocable – Not possible to revoke. Unalterable.

Power – The ability to act or produce an effect.

Thought – The action or process of thinking. A product of thinking or serious consideration.

* Concept/Objective: Thoughts have an amazing ability to produce, in no limit of time, that which is thought about. Fleeting thoughts are one thing, but when we entertain thoughts they will eventually manifest themselves in our lives. Be mindful of the types of thoughts you have. Control your thoughts and control your destiny.

(Questions)

1. Why are the types of thoughts you have so important?
2. Where do thoughts come from and how are they formed?
3. Why is the world devoid of really great thinkers?

Whether you realize it or not, what you think about matters. Your thoughts hold great sway over how you feel. They hold great sway over who and what you attract in your life. And they hold great sway over how you behave. Your thoughts are so powerful that a mere single thought has the ability to transform you into itself. They simply contain the amazing ability to produce into your life that which is at the core of your thoughts. It does this almost irrevocably. This is the power you have just by how you think. So, if you think that how you think or what you think about does not matter, then you are in for a rude awakening.

Nothing that you will ever do or feel is independent of thought. Whether it be conscious or otherwise. The types of thoughts you have are so important that you have to even think about what you think about. Because if a large part of your thinking is focused on inconsequential things, then this thinking will take you away from what you should be thinking about, and invariably they will take you away from your desired goals and move you in the direction of your predominant thoughts. This is not the case with fleeting thoughts. The question now becomes why do you have the types of thoughts you have? And more importantly, where do thoughts come from?

I think it is safe to say that thoughts just don't pop up out of thin air. So where do they come from?

Thoughts are materially based. And if thoughts are materially based, then what material forms the basis of the thoughts you have? Where does this material come from? How is it produced? If someone says, 'hey, I didn't mean to make you feel that way', and we said earlier that thoughts hold great sway over how you feel, then thought precedes feelings or mood. Let's look at these thoughts and what gives them the power to produce certain feelings or how they contribute to putting you in a certain mood.

It's been said many times that thought is the cause of it all. Thought is first. And your senses are the doorway by which enters the activating agents that form the basis of the material that will become your thoughts. Each sense is a different doorway. And each doorway produces a different effect. And each effect can produce very specific feelings, actions, viewpoints, and so on. Just think about how you feel right this moment. Or how you felt at some point in the past. What made you feel that way? Was it something you experienced through your senses? I would say yes.

While we are here, I think it is necessary to comment on the value of experiences. It is not always what you experience that is important, but how you experience what you experience and how you allow it to affect you is perhaps even more important. More on this in another card. Let's get back to these senses.

If, for example, I smell a sweet perfume, or I hear some bad news, or I feel the warm rays of the sun on a cool day, or I taste something salty, or I watch my child take its first steps; each of these will have a different effect on my mood and how I feel, and in turn a thought or series of thoughts will come up in succession which will reflect itself in my feelings, my actions and how I look at things.

Your eyes, ears, tongue, nose and skin are your five sense organs. These are the doorways I spoke of earlier. What you experience through each of these senses not only causes a conscious and immediate effect, but even a lingering and delayed subconscious response that might not take form until sometime in the distant future when called upon through certain experiences.

This is how powerful thoughts are and this is why you have to constantly assess what you think about because of the effect they can have on you. Guard your thoughts. If you notice an errant thought, eradicate it. If you notice a thought that is irrational, cast it aside. The key thing is not to entertain certain thoughts. Not that you are not going to think about certain things, that's not the problem. It's when those thoughts are allowed to take up residence in your mind, that is when things can become problematic.

Once you have been exposed to various stimuli by way of your senses, which then becomes material for your thoughts, then this material is dormant until called upon. Time and circumstances bring to surface that which is within you. Hardly is there anyone who is an independent thinker. Most thoughts that anyone has is an amalgamation of a consortium of things taken in throughout their life. Even when confronted with having to make a decision, and someone tries to interject to give the other some advice, you will often hear the phrase, "I want to handle this on my own, I want to do my own thinking." I would tell that person good luck with that.

Whatever decision they arrive at, supposedly 'on their own', was greatly influenced by things past. Anything they ever saw, anything they ever heard, or anything they ever felt in their life pulled on this inner material to form a thought. This could be as simple as a commercial they saw ten years earlier in which a product was being advertised to be sold. Not being aware of this subliminal programming, they carry with them on the subconscious level a thought, an idea, or an opinion, by inference.

The key thing is the insertion of someone else's thoughts and ideas. Once there, time and circumstance are all that is needed to influence future decisions. Now multiply this by an almost incalculable number that indicates everything that you have ever taken in by your senses throughout your life. So no, any thought that you ever have is never solely yours. Don't be deluded into thinking it is. Although it is exclusively tied to you and is made and expressed uniquely because of the uniqueness of every individual.

The world is devoid of really great thinkers in part because of what the vast majority of people mentally consume. Such terms as garbage in garbage out, and you are what you eat applies here. If what you see, what you hear, and what you feel is under the control of others, then your thoughts can be manipulated to embody the interests of someone else and not yours.

When your thoughts have become heavily influenced by these negative outside forces that don't have your best interest at heart, then you can be duped into thinking that your thoughts are yours. When in fact there has been an unfriendly invasion. Your mind has become poisoned by the thoughts and ideas of others. Your thoughts have become diluted very craftily and very subtly which cages your mind. You become locked into a thought pattern that can only carry you so far.

It might be a stretch of the imagination for some to think that others can train your brain in such a way that it thinks against itself. And it may be a bold proclamation, but it is one I very strongly believe in. And if you examined yourself enough, and tried to understand why you think the way you do, you will soon discover a startling reality. Then you will be forced to concede that you have been masterfully manipulated.

It shouldn't be surprising then that a lot of people think only within the confines of the box they have been placed in. Venture out. Explore. Question everything you have ever learned. Examine yourself and how you think. Do your thoughts reflect that which is in your best interest. If not, then that is evidence of a foreign intruder that must be ousted. It is not natural to think and act against yourself. That type of thinking and acting is irrational.

This is another way of saying you are not in your right mind. The question becomes, why not? There is always a cause. So what and who caused this irrationality of thought? You have to realize that it is so deceptively power to be able to engineer your way into another's subconscious mind and root yourself there. It is so deceptively powerful to maliciously contribute to the false, negative, and deceptive imagery that you know others will see and ingest. To set up systems that you know will ill effect many in that system. The bottom line is that we feed from ancient and warped minds in a multitude of ways whose thoughts we unknowingly consume and reflect.

Even the circumstances that played a large part in many of the base experiences you ever went through must be examined as well. You can label this anything you want to, but all I'm getting at here is that you need to study your mind. Your mind is the engine that powers everything you think and do. And if it is in any way out of whack then there are some much needed repairs that need to happen if you want to harness and direct the power of your own being.

To be a great thinker you must be a critical thinker. Analyze whatever you are being confronted with. It won't be easy because like we discussed previously, a massive amount of craft and skill was and is being used to bypass your conscious mind. You will be astonished at the level of trickery being employed, and at best this will cause you to never swallow anything again hook, line, and sinker.

The real power of your mind is directly connected to how you think and what you think about. Change your thoughts and you will change your life. The more frequently you think about certain thoughts, they will develop a specific frequency. The higher the thoughts, the higher the frequency, and the higher the frequency, the more powerful your mind will become. By elevating your thoughts, and growing more powerful in that regard, you will produce a greater ability to draw from that which is around you.

Your entire life is a big reflection of what types of thoughts have dominated your mind. In order to have power over your mind and your thoughts, and invariably your life, there must be a reduction of what you have been taking in that is not good for you. Never think that you are powerless in any aspect of your life because you are not. And don't underestimate the irrevocable power of thought.

* Key Points:
    a. What you think about matters
    b. Thoughts are materially based
    c. Your senses are the doorway by which enters the activating agents that form the basis of the material from which your thoughts are produced
    d. Your thoughts will always manifest themselves in your life
    e. There is no thought that is exclusively yours
    f. Examine yourself and how you think

Card 17: Adversarial Companionship

Adversary - One that contends with, opposes, or resists: An enemy.

Adversity - A state or instance of serious or continued difficulty or misfortune.

Companion - A person or thing that accompanies another. To keep company.

* Concept/Objective: Growing pains are painful for a reason. They aid you in your growth. You must develop an intimate relationship with hurt, pain, and suffering. Let them accompany you to greatness. Resist seeking the path of least resistance.

(Questions)
1. Is there a need for adversity in your life? Why or why not?
2. Why does pressure bring out the best in people?
3. Why do people, for the most part, seek the path of least resistance?

"Understanding how to surmount pain, doubt, and failure is a vital component in winning the game of life. So often we are concerned with what makes us feel good that we forget about what makes us great. Character is not made out of sunshine and roses. Like steel, it is forged in fire, between the hammer and the anvil." 5

Pain and suffering are precursors to greatness. They should be embraced. Obviously no one wants to suffer. Nevertheless the checks and balances in nature dictate that to achieve a certain level of success or greatness there needs to be a corresponding and equivalent work that is accompanied by great pain, suffering, and adversity. Pain, in this sense, is your best friend. Your faithful companion that will never leave your side. So why not get to know her? Why not develop an intimate relationship with pain? It is only when you know pain on a personal level that you will begin to appreciate her. At this point you will no longer see pain as some strange thing that is meant to hurt or punish you. She will gently nudge you onward and upward if you will let her do her job.

You will never know greatness until you know pain. They both are dependent upon the other. The more you increase your threshold for pain, the more you increase your potential for greatness. Pain definitely is a dark place. But fret not because this is in accord with the natural order of things. Darkness is the place where all life has its beginnings. But it doesn't stay there, if it is to evolve that is. Be careful not to be suffocated by your relationship with pain and the dark places that it can take you. It is only a temporary, yet necessary stage each of us must cyclically go through.

Adversities are difficulties. How will any of us ever know what we are made of unless and until difficult circumstances are allowed to bring whatever is in us out? Most of us have never been taught that difficulties and adversity bring out the best in us. That they build character. They will, and they do, if we embrace them and don't shrink from them. Your value and worth are beyond measure, but you will never know it without adversity. Without Difficulties.

The road to greatness is beset with difficulties. It always has been. But that road is not traveled by the vast majority of the human family. Most people seek the path of least resistance. But why seek the path of least resistance, where there is little to no difficulty factor? No adversity? No pressure? Without any of these three, the best of you will remain buried deep within.

Study the lives of great people. I mean the really great ones. All we see is what we see, the end result. What we don't see is the behind the scenes of what they had to go through to get to where they eventually arrived at. Most of them struggled, suffered, and worked hard. If we were acquainted with all the rejection, setbacks, or losses they experienced we would see that they paid a heck of a price to get to where they eventually ended up. Had they turned their back in the face of their struggles they never would have been molded or forged into the specimen they grew into. Adversity is a road less traveled. But it is the way to unimaginable heights.

"We have certainly created man to face difficulties." [11]

Seeking the path of least resistance is never the best course of action. It is understandable that anyone would have a natural aversion to pain. For who in their right mind would be willing to throw themselves into the throes of affliction of their own volition? Who doesn't want to live a life of ease? Living a life of ease has hidden dangers though. It weakens instead of strengthens. It erodes character. It spoils and rots us from within. We become unfit for life and incapable of dealing with the problems that come with life.

Ease is good for us, but only after difficulty. Ease is never first. Difficulty is. They both come in cycles one after the other. Over and over and over. You see, this is growing pains. No pain equals no growth. If you are content, then live life as you have. But if you want to qualify for more, then you have to be willing to take more. Don't settle for less than what you rightfully deserve. You get what you strive for, and striving takes effort.

Is all suffering and adversity good? There is a spark of good in all suffering no matter how it comes our way. However, we can suffer naturally or unnaturally. Meaning, through ignorance, we bring misfortune in our lives unnecessarily. This is what is meant by unnatural suffering. When you do what is right, and you suffer as a result, that's one thing; But when you suffer from doing other than right, that's an altogether different thing. No matter where you are in your life at this moment, no matter what you may be going through, you can grow from it. Muster up all the strength you can to come out on top. This is how you turn a negative into a positive.

* **Key Points:**
    a. Pain and suffering is a precursor to greatness
    b. Difficult circumstances allow you to see what you are made of
    c. Difficulties and adversities build character
    d. Seeking the path of least resistance is never the best course of action
    e. No pain equals no growth

f. There is a spark of good in all suffering no matter how it comes our way

Card 18: Preparing for All Eventualities

Prepare – To make ready beforehand for some purpose or use. To work out the details of. To plan in advance.

All – The whole amount: Entire. As much as possible.

Eventuality – A possible event or outcome: Possibility.

* Concept/Objective: No one in a world like this can afford to be careless. There is no excuse for being unprepared for any event. It should be a crime to leave things to chance. Anything foreseeable is worthy of giving the proper attention to. Nothing is more dangerous than being caught off guard or left in the lurch.

(Questions)
1. When should you apply the wait and see approach?
2. What is the key to being prepared for all eventualities?
3. What should your preparation entail in any given situation?

The wait and see approach has its time and place. When something has not yet taken place, and there is a degree of uncertainty about how it can turn out, then it is best to wait and see. You use this time to think, to anticipate, and to prepare. There is safety in this approach. However, when something has already been put in motion and it can't be changed or undone, then nature has to run its course. There is nothing to be done. All you can do is wait and see what happens. Even in these cases you look at each possible outcome of that event and make tentative preparations for each possible outcome.

There are also occasions when you do have the ability to alter an event, but you make this decision, after careful deliberation, that it would be unwise to intercede. So you wait and see. You stay out the fray. This is more commonly seen in situations where you are caught in the middle of a situation where no matter what side you choose, the end result would be less than promising either way.

Because of this foresight, you decide to sit on the sidelines. Unless and until things are getting out of hand or things have progressed to a certain point that your involvement is not only needed, but necessary, and to not get involved would only exacerbate things. In those cases, you don't wait and see. To wait and see in these types of situations can cause more harm than good. Why relinquish control of any situation and leave it in the hands of others or to chance when it is in your power to exercise control and manipulate the outcome in your favor.

Anything that can happen has a likelihood of

happening. This is when the law of probability becomes relevant. The law of probability, in this sense, refers to your knowledge surrounding all the circumstances that exists of an event's chances of happening or not happening. Any circumstance that you have knowledge of qualifies as a probable event. Events are usually precipitated by conditions and circumstances. When you know of a condition or a circumstance, then you are being provided with the possibility of formulating plans that can prevent unfavorable outcomes. You can't predict everything. Some things are simply unpredictable. If it were possible to make iron clad predictions, then nothing that ever went wrong would have gone wrong.

It is virtually impossible to prepare for every unknown eventuality, except that you cover as many potential happenings as possible. These preparations are in the form of contingencies. Your contingency planning will deal with a lot of what ifs. You must workout, in your mind, different scenarios and your responses to those scenarios should they occur, as can be seen in the following:

"...Among the commendations which Philopoemon, Prince of the Achaians, has received from historians is this—that in times of peace he was always thinking of methods of warfare, so that when walking in the country with his friends he would often stop and talk with them on the subject.

'If the enemy, 'he would say,' were posted on that hill, and we found ourselves here with our army, which of us would have the better position? How would we most safely and in the best order advance to meet him? If we had to retreat, what direction should we take? If they retired, how should we pursue? In this way he put to his friends, as he went along, all the contingencies that can befall an army. He listened to their opinions, stated his own, and supported them with reasons; and from his being constantly occupied with such meditations, it resulted, that when in actual command no complication could ever present itself with which he was not prepared to deal'." 7

Always prepare for worst case scenarios. There are only a limited number of ways in which a thing can turn out. For you, against you, or things can remain unchanged. Anything in your favor is good and no preparation at all is necessary because that is the best case scenario. That which is unchanged only needs a slight nudge to tilt things in your favor. Which means coming up with ways to accomplish that. However, your main attention must be focused on absolutely anything that can go wrong. Because it is only that which can go wrong that can hurt you, as we've discussed elsewhere.

Stay alert and aware to different variables that can change things in an instant. Always remain in a state of readiness. Never be caught off guard. No matter what you are engaged in, be it at work, at home, or during some leisure time activity; consciously be alert and aware to surrounding threats. You see it in nature all the time. Study the meerkat for example. Someone is always on guard to alert the others of impending dangers or threats. It is second nature to them. Why shouldn't you be expected to operate from a higher form of safety and awareness?

'Proper preparation is only possible with knowledge of conditions for or against which preparation is being made.'   1

* **Key Points:**
    a. The wait and see approach has its time and place
    b. Have contingencies in place to deal with possible events
    c. Events are precipitated by conditions and circumstances
    d. Stay alert and aware to different variables
    e. Prepare for everything conceivably possible

Card 19: Insultive Indulgences

Insult - To treat with insolence, indignity, or contempt. To offend.

Indulge - To give free reign to. To treat with excessive leniency.

* Concept/Objective: Some things in life you must

learn to put up with. Other things you must never put up with. Being able to differentiate between the two is important. Life is full of people who lack good table manners. People who are just plain rude. From such, stay way.

(Questions)
1. Why must you learn how to take an insult?
2. When should an insult be taken as an insult?
3. What should all this say about your own manners?

"Sometimes society imposes insults that must be borne, be comforted of course by the knowledge that there will come a time when the most humble of men, if he keeps his eyes open, can take his revenge on even the most powerful. It is this knowledge that prevented the Don from losing the humility all his friends admired in him." 8

If you don't learn how to take an insult in life you will always find yourself in conflict. Too much conflict is not good. Remember, you are attempting to master your own reality and directing the course of your life in the direction that you choose to take it. But if you always have to respond to petty offenses or trivial insults then they will keep you embroiled in one thing after another. This will only take you in the opposite direction that your energy and attention should be focused on.

So, responding to every insult can take its toll. How? It's simple physics. Every action brings about an opposite and equal reaction. Never be pulled into something not of your own choosing. Consider how your response can have a snowball effect. Multiply your own actions by another's response to get a reading on certain probable outcomes. By seeing the end in advance, you will be provided with the insight necessary to know how or if you should respond. And if so, how you should respond. Sometimes the fox isn't worth the chase.

Knowing how one thing can lead to another will dictate any course of action on your part after carefully weighing everything out. You have to maintain control of your destiny at all times. The slightest thing can make all the difference. Whether it be in thought or action. Every insult does not deserve a response. Incivility is rampant and can be found almost anywhere and in everyone. This position should not be taken as an excuse to be a doormat. That is not what is being driven at here. You only take this position to avoid insignificant squabbles that in all truth, doesn't warrant your attention. As the saying goes, 'you have bigger fish to fry.'.

Sometimes, however, enough is enough. You only have two cheeks. How many times can you turn them? There are times when you have to call people out. You do this when people take your meekness for weakness. You do this without ever getting outside of yourself. When someone offends you, it can take you to a place that is dark and gloomy. How people act is not in your control, but how you respond is. In your response is the determining factor for how things unfold for you from that point forward. You have more power in this dynamic than you realize.

Always maintain control. In doing this you control when, where, how, or even if you respond. Some responses are more immediate and necessary than others. If something has to be addressed in the moment, don't hesitate. Let necessity be your guide. Whether you bide your time or not, you wait because you can, not because you have to. Your thought process has now evolved to the point where you now put everything on a scale and weigh its relative importance. Modeling and matching how you deal with it factoring in even the smallest of details.

"A brother offended is harder to be won than a strong city: and their contentions are like the bars of a castle.". 10

Everyone does not take offenses and insults the same way. Be careful who you offend. Extend to all men their proper respect. Rubbing the wrong person the wrong way can have dire consequences. Some people take the smallest thing as an insult. What's more alarming is that if they are of this breed, you won't know you've done anything wrong until it is too late. It is virtually impossible to go through life without ever offending anyone. It is going to happen.

When it happens, let it be incidental rather from outright disregard for the other person.

There will be times when you are purposefully brash. Let the specifics of the situation call for it. Who you insult matters in these instances. Disregard the wrong person's standing to your own peril if you want to. Just be prepared for the worst. You will become a passion of theirs. If they didn't have a purpose for their life, you just gave them one. They will spend the rest of their life trying to get even. No one can serve a colder dish than someone offended, wronged, or crossed. Even if you do happen to offend someone, and they profess forgiveness, be ever mindful of your trespass. People may forgive, but they don't forget. You mustn't either. Be aware of any subtle attempt for them to exact revenge or get even somehow.

"Any harm you do to a man should be done in such a way that you need not fear his revenge.". 3

* Key Points:
- a. In life you have to learn how to take an insult
- b. Always keep your long range goals in mind
- c. There should be a limit to how much you take from others
- d. Extend to all men their proper respect
- e. Be prepared for the worst when you offend others

Card 20: The Royal Crown Affair

Royal - Suitable for royalty. Regal character or bearing.

Crown - The highest part. The topmost part of the skull or head.

Affair - Matter. Concern.

* Concept/Objective: If you want to be crowned all you need to do is be royal in your own fashion. And others will bestow upon you the best of everything. Heavy is the head that wears the crown, but so are the rewards. Aren't you worth your weight in gold? Act like it. Power does not come without a price.

(Questions)
1. What makes you worthy to be crowned?
2. Is royalty a thing of the past?
3. Why is heavy is the head that wears the crown?

"The Crown. Place it upon your head and you assume a different pose—tranquil yet radiating assurance. Never show doubt, never lose your dignity beneath the crown, or it will not fit. It will seem destined for one more worthy. Do not wait for a coronation; the greatest emperors crown themselves." [2]

Your worth should always be determined by you, never by anyone else. The lens that you use to measure your worth should be through your own eyes. Any other measuring tool is incapable of giving you an accurate description of your true value or worth. You were born worthy to receive the best of what this world has to offer. Somehow somewhere along the way we have been stripped of our rendezvous with our true destiny because of a faulty self-concept that has destroyed any hope or expectation within us of anything more than what we have or where we are. This diminished view of ourselves must give way to a grander one.

Now, based upon this, don't you think that your worthiness should be a matter of concern to you? This affair, the royal crown affair, is one of supreme importance because it reintroduces you to your greatness. So to properly discuss the royal crown affair is to discuss your natural born right to be the beneficiary of everything your heart desires by equipping you with a mindset of a god and of a ruler.

The only thing that will ever be kept from you is that which you are not ready to receive. The crown is yours to wear if you so desire to place it, not on your head, but in your head. And this is what will produce around you an aura that is godlike. This invisible halo results from the knowledge that has been put in the crown of your head, which is unseen, but not unfelt. As you can see, this is not your traditional crown.

Knowing and seeing what others don't makes you king in a land where ignorance and blindness is rampant and in abundance. When you know what others don't know, and are able to see what others can't see, then you are able to rule. But this is only part of it. The larger part of it deals with self-image and behavioral characteristics. How you see yourself and how you act are the most important things when it comes to you being worthy to be crowned.

This first starts in your mind, then in the minds of others. How you see yourself matters. How you act and treat yourself matters as well. Self-image is portrayed to more than just yourself, it is reflected in your overall mannerisms and in all your dealings with anyone that you come in contact with. How you act and treat yourself affects how others act towards you. This leads to the respect factor.

Without respect, you are ruined and will never become powerful enough to be crowned. All respect begins with you respecting yourself. Don't ever mistreat yourself and you must never permit another to treat you below your worthy state. Respect is commanded, never demanded. Only the weak demand respect. It must be commanded by virtue of your bearing. Your commanding presence dictates how you are seen and treated by others. And this is why how you carry yourself is crucial. This will also produce in you a confidence, not to be confused with arrogance, that will become infectious and have a big impact on others.

Some think that royalty is a thing of the past, if you are one that thinks the same, then the only thing that will be a relic of the past is you. Times change, people change, and nothing ever stays the same; but history has a way of repeating itself. It's cyclical. Things have a way of coming full circle. That which you lost in the past is being offered right back to you in the present. The question is, will you accept it?

The heaviness of the crown is the weight of the knowledge you have to carry and the associated responsibilities that come with it. Power comes with a price tag attached to it. And this is why you should never sell yourself short. Never accept anything less than what you deserve. Regality knows nothing other than the best of everything. The level you place yourself own is a level you must not descend from no matter what. So don't stoop to any level that is beneath you for any reason. Your dignity won't allow it anyway. Lowering your standards is dangerous and will most definitely work against you in your ascension to the throne.

Lastly, of all the beings that exist on the planet, none are higher than the human being. You see, this is what we have been saying all along, you are already supreme, you are already the best, and you are already the greatest, you just didn't know it. You are a supreme being. You were destined to rule and to govern. But you will continue to act other than yourself because you only know other than yourself. Your greatness, in terms of you displaying it, will unfold at a rate commensurate to the revelation you receive about yourself. This is, no doubt, an affair of great resolution, a royal crown affair.

* Key Points:
  a. Your worth should always be determined by you, never by anyone else
  b. People will treat you how you act and how you treat yourself
  c. The only thing that will ever be kept from you is that which you are not ready to receive
  d. Confidence, not arrogance, should be your hallmark
  e. Respect is commanded, never demanded
  f. Heavy has always been the head that wears the crown because it is laden with heavy responsibilities

Card 21: The Undeniable Power of Magnetism

Undeniable - Plainly true. Incontestable. Unquestionable.

Magnetic - Possessing an extraordinary power or ability to attract. Of or relating to a magnet or magnetism.

Magnetism - The ability to attract or charm.

* Concept/Objective: If you want to have power over things in your life, you must control who and what you attract to you. You are a human magnet with the ability to attract to you whoever and whatever you like. You do it all the time, why not do it con-

sciously? You will never be denied what you have in your mind, it will come to you no matter what.

(Questions)
1. What is the law of attraction?
2. How can you become a magnet of power?
3. Is there such a thing as attracting and/or being attracted to the wrong thing?

"Everything that's coming into your life you are attracting into your life. And it's attracted to you by virtue of the images you're holding in your mind...Whatever is going on in your mind you are attracting to you." [13]

Like attracts like. This is the law of attraction. Once you learn the simple science behind this law, there will never be a reason for you to ever wonder why your condition is the way it is. Whatever you have in your life, you attracted it to you. This includes the type of people you meet, the condition of your life, and the opportunities that cross your path. All of this is connected to what you have in your mind, the strength of your character, and the principles you live your life by.

Mind you, none of this is to say that you are the cause of or deserving of everything bad that happens in your life, because like they say, bad things sometimes happen to good people. This is a fact of life. It also neither absolves those who purposefully cast a wide net to capture the unwitting ones for selfish gain. Even still, that net would not be as effective in snaring you if your level of mind and thought patterns put you out of its general reach. However, whenever this is allowed to happen, it is because there is a superior law at work that serves a greater purpose that may be unknown to you on the level of mind you are presently operating from.

Notwithstanding, a large percentage of people are unaware of this universal law working in their life. This is why ignorance must be fought against wherever it exists in your mind. And this is why I believe it says, "My people are destroyed for the lack of knowledge..." 10; and for no other reason than that. You should always be found striving to become as intimately acquainted with any knowledge that can lift you up and help you to change your present condition.

Did you know or do you believe that your heavenly state or condition awaits only you? The type of thoughts that you constantly think about the most can either foster and bring up your latent and sublime qualities, or they can inhibit and retard their growth, and thereby either drawing good things to you or keeping them at bay. But the more you elevate your thinking you will become that much more attractive and your magnetic field or influence is expanded to reach more people and objects that are reflective of those thoughts.

Your life is only a mirror of your predominant thoughts and feelings. Too many times we find ways to externalize the source of our problems or miserable condition. Everything begins and ends with you. You can only control you, no one else. When you harbor ill will towards someone else, whether it's justified or not, it will always cost you more than the other person. It could be jealousy, anger, or even hatred, it doesn't matter. Who does these feelings affect the most? That's right, you.

These emotional thoughts destroy you from within. Remember, whatever we have in our mind, we will bring in our life in some form or fashion. Get rid of any self-destructive thoughts and replace them immediately with thoughts that are more in line with what you truly desire for yourself. The law of attraction is real and you will undeniably draw to you whatever is in your mind.

"The Magnet. An unseen force that draws objects to it, which in turn becomes magnetized themselves, drawing other pieces to them, the magnetic power of the whole constantly increasing. But take away the original magnet and it all falls apart. Become the magnet, the invisible force that attracts..." 2

Did you know or do you believe that you can amass so must attracting power that people and things will gravitate to you even against their will? There will be something so alluring about you that you will be like a magnet drawing others to you. In order to do this, you yourself have to become magnetized. Others will be drawn to you because you radiate or give off a frequency that they themselves are trying to tune into. But you are already there. Like minds will always find a way to connect with other like minds. No matter the differing levels of mind, their similarities cause them to be attracted to one another.

Magnetism is an element of what is called an electromagnetic force. This is the forcefield that is produced by magnets that is considered a phenomenon that causes things to either be attracted to or repelled from a magnetic source. Anything that falls within that magnetic field becomes magnetized itself. This magnetization is depended upon mainly three factors such as the magnitude of the charge in the field, the velocity or speed of matter or particles in the magnetic field, and the strength of the magnetic field itself.

There are things about you that will be both appealing and non-appealing to others no matter what level of mind you operate from or whatever thought pattern governs your thinking. Naturally we attract and will be attracted to that which we think about the most. And this is why we only see what we want to see, we only hear what we want to hear, and we only think about what we think about. But we can also be attracted to and attract things that are not necessarily good to us or for us.

You've heard the phrase, 'like moths to a flame'. Have you ever wondered why moths are attracted to or drawn to flames? Well, it isn't necessarily the flame itself as much as it is the light source that draws them towards it. This could be any innocuous or harmless light from a porch light, street light, or a flashlight. Or it can be drawn to a light, such as flames that are emitted from bonfires or fireplaces. The latter of these lights, if the moths get to close, could not only be harmful, but deadly. This attraction is more of an urge because moths see the light as something desirable, not that they contain any magnetic properties in the ordinary sense of a real magnet. But they do have powers of attraction over moths.

Somehow, like the moth, we are unable to distinguish between good light or bad light, or good people and good things or bad people and bad things. Yet, sometimes we can distinguish, but the attracting power of the person or thing overrides our logical thought process. To our own detriment of course.

As you can see, we not only can pull people and things to us, we can also be pulled in by other people and other things as well. You have to be aware of both of the ways the law of attraction works. Especially if the outside magnetic force is stronger than yours. If so, stay away from its magnetic field of influence that it can have over you. Get too close and you may be sucked in. Don't forget to remember how magnetic forces are undeniable. Don't tempt yourself in that way.

Just know that you should never ignore or underestimate your powers of attraction that are always at work in your life. It is much better to control what you attract than attracting things unintentionally. You do this by controlling what you think about. And by only thinking about what you want or need in your life. Nothing else should really be a concern to you. Stop letting frivolous things occupy your mind because those thoughts or feelings will only bring more of the same into your life.

* Key Points:
    a. Like attracts like is the simple yet powerful law of attraction
    b. Whatever you have in your life, you attracted it to you
    c. Under very specific conditions you are not always the cause of or deserving of everything bad that happens in your life because sometimes bad things do happen to good people
    d. You have more power than you think when it comes to producing for yourself a heavenly state or condition
    e. Your life is only a mirror of your predominant thoughts and feelings.

f. Like minds will always find a way to connect with other like minds

g. Be as equally careful of who or what you are attracted to as those who you attract

Card 22: Team Building

Team - To put together in a coordinated ensemble or manner. A number of people brought together to form a particular work or activity. A cohesive unit or group that is bound by a common goal or interest.

Build - To develop according to a systematic plan, on a particular basis. To construct and form into a whole.

* Concept/Objective: Know the keys to putting together a winning team. Put aces in their places. Have well established standards that are enforceable. Unify them around clearly defined goals that are attainable. Create an atmosphere of trust that is unshakable. Do this and you have discovered the lynchpins to building a strong and effective team.

(Questions)

1. How can you ensure that you have assembled the best team possible?
2. What should be the criteria for team building that ensures the cohesiveness and continued progressiveness of the unit?

3. What is another word for team that describes it in a more intimate way?

By getting the best and most qualified people available, you have the material to produce the best team. An inferior quality product, no matter the product, is a sure means of producing the opposite effect no matter what you are building. Assembling a team is no different. This is just the starting point. Once your team has been assembled, now you have to put your team in the best possible position to win. How is this accomplished? Proper people placement, comprehensive and effective training, and have in place clearly defined agreed upon goals. These are the three pillars of team building.

The first pillar of team building is proper placement of team members. This is so important to a fluid operation that it must be underscored here. You will only be setting that team member up for failure by putting them in a position that they are ill equipped to function in at an optimal level. The secret to knowing where to place your people is if it is in line with their natural abilities. To do otherwise is both unwise and a sure means of not getting the most out of that station, not to mention the potential for failure we just mentioned above.

"To send people to war without teaching them is called abandoning them...first train them in conduct and duty, teach them to be loyal and trustworthy, instruct them in rules and penalties...". 1

Training that is comprehensive and effective is the second pillar of team building. Seems simple enough, but it is oftentimes neglected to some extent. Being thorough in teaching and training accounts for nothing if the result of that teaching and training does not produce effectiveness in that team member. How can you tell if it is effective? By the output of production and in those situations that brings that teaching and training to bear.

The third and last pillar of team building is having clearly defined goals. Direction is critical. Everyone needs to know without any ambiguity what the team's goals are. This also needs to be accompanied by an understanding that that team member is in agreement with the direction the team is headed in. Having a common consensus lessens the drag that is produced by non-compliant members. It serves no one well to have an unshared vision by members of your team. Everyone needs to buy in, otherwise they are not a good fit.

The selection process is a very discriminating one and only those who possess a very specific skill set should even be considered. The selection process may seem like the beginning, but it is only a means to gather the right personnel to facilitate the manifestation or furtherance of a previously conceived idea. As is the case in most instances, the core person or persons who are a part of the original idea are more connected to it than others who join in at some future time. Since the core members are more acquainted with the inner dynamics of where the idea or team is headed, they are the most qualified to assess the qualifications of possible additions to the team and are the only ones entrusted to do so.

The team picks you to be a part of it and not the other way around. The entrusted ones have the heavy responsibility of picking those who fit snugly into the overall concept, purpose, and function of the team. They are qualified to look for those qualities, traits, characteristics, and abilities, and other intangibles that are essential to them performing in a manner that is commensurate with the objectives of the team.

"The commander must be wise, trustful, benevolent, courageous, and strict." 6

A very high standard of excellence is always expected and maintained. This brings us to one of the most critical points, that of good leadership. Everything starts at the top. You can't hold others accountable when you are derelict. Good leadership involves the ability to produce in those under their leadership an unshakable trust in them and you in them. To be able to provide vision and purpose for the team. To effectively eradicate divisiveness and harmoniously unify the members of the team. Coercion is not effective in the long run, so it is rarely, if ever, applied. Nothing is to be forced. But once certain things are put in place, the structure and integrity of the team must be enforced by strict measures. None of this can happen without substantive leadership.

Another word for team is family. Your team is your family. There is nothing more important than family, so there is nothing more important than your team. Any other way of looking at your team is not a proper way. Not much needs to be said about this. The term family speaks for itself.

* Key Points:
- a. By getting the best and most qualified people, you have what it takes to build a winning team
- b. The three pillars of team building are; Proper people placement, comprehensive and effective training, and having clearly defined agreed upon goals
- c. Set high enforceable standards
- d. Have an invitation only policy
- e. Good leadership is essential to team building
- f. Another word for team is family

Card 23: Interrogatories

Interrogate - To question formally or systematically. Inquisitive.

* Concept/Objective: The first thing to understand when being questioned is the motive of the questioner.

All questions have answers, but this does not mean you should be the one to give the answer. Questions are like hooks with worms. They contain hidden dangers and traps. So, beware.

(Questions)
1. What is the generally recognized purpose of interrogations?
2. In what way can you retrieve more than you leave from a highly skilled interrogator?
3. What accounts for a person's unwavering ability to remain unflinching in the face of a barrage of questions even when the questioner knows they are being lied to?

No matter what surface reason is given, usually when a person is being interrogated it carries with it a hidden purpose that is unknown to the one being interrogated until some distance in the future. This distance can be measured in seconds or minutes, or it could take months or years. The effects of these interrogations can be measured similarly, depending of course on certain factors. Wide ranging questions are a major part of investigations. There are times when an answer is known prior to or when a question is asked? At other times this is not the case.

In the case of the former, verification, corroboration, or entrapment is the goal. The latter, which covers a bevy of reasons during interrogations, unknown information is being sought after. In a nutshell, interrogators, investigators, or inspectors are after information that will aid them in some way. And if this information helps them, what do you think that information will do to you? You have no incentive to speak to any interrogator. Let them do their job some other way.

If you are not used to being professionally questioned or interrogated it can be a very daunting and intimidating experience. Nervousness is usually associated in these types of settings even if you have nothing to hide or haven't done anything wrong. Investigators play on this much anticipated feeling or condition. It is hard to think straight when you are fearful or nervous and they know this. Especially if you are a novice. Just keep in mind that anything you say can and will be used against you. Always protect yourself from self-incrimination. You have rights. The right to remain silent. Exercise that right.

Scrutinize all prying minds unapologetically. When you find yourself in the hot seat so to speak, turn the tables on your would-be interrogators by asking them questions. This will serve a dual purpose. For one, it will force your interrogators to reveal more than what they intended. And two, it will cause them to get less from you than what they expected. How is this accomplished?

Simple. Question them on the questions they ask you by having their questions explained. All under the guise of needing clarification so you can better understand their questions. "What do you mean by that?", What does that have to do with me?", "I don't quite understand how that has to do with anything?", "I don't see how I can help you in that matter?", etcetera. Once they clarify or explain they will be careful not to give you too much, but they will give you just enough for you to get a glimpse into their motives for questioning you in the first place, in some cases even more.

At the end of which you can answer, should you choose to, any number of ways. Yes, no, I don't know, or whatever. As long as the answer does not hurt you in any way. You get more. They get less. Be careful because how you question your questioners can also give them insight too. Unless you are skilled in the art of counter interrogation, and aware of certain legal points that can snare you, then it is best to shy away from this approach and leave it to the professionals by seeking legal counsel or simply remaining silent.

Remember, these people are professionally trained. So much so that you even have to be careful who you share sensitive information with, even if they are trustworthy. You want to protect them and ultimately yourself because wise interrogators can elicit information in the subtlest of ways. The truth of any matter, if it is possessed by anyone, even if they don't verbally confirm this that or the other, they still reveal things in how they deny.

Beyond facial expressions and body language, there are always subtle cues that are discernible by trained minds. How a person says no can let investigators know that they hit on something and are on the right track. Leads can be confirmed or developed this way. And always remember, it is never what they know, it's what they can prove. So always deny, deny, deny. Even in the face of threats, say nothing. Even if you are promised something, say nothing. Because of the severity of the matter it bears repeating, what you say can and will be used against you. Most cases would never be solved unless information is provided in some form. Don't let you be the one to provide this information.

Even in your ordinary everyday life people are always probing, trying to sift you. Whether directly or indirectly. Presume no question is innocent. Always search out the motive of any question that hits your ears. This can be done silently or aloud. Silent searches will cause you to be stingy with your words in response. Aloud you can simply ask, "what do you mean by that?", "where did that come from?", "why does that matter?", or, "who told you that?". What you say is in direct proportion to what is asked of you. The goal is to have what is being asked of you explained, thereby exposing its roots.

To do this you must learn how to question widely to get the specific information you are looking for. Finding out who, what, when, where, how, and why will provide you with the identity, it will distinguish between things, provide you with the timing of something, let you know the place, learn the means or method, and uncover the reasoning or motive.

By doing this, it can provide you with a full range of information that will give you a clearer picture of any situation. When someone is conveying information to you let them speak all the way through without any interruptions. Then at the end you can ask questions for clarification. Look for inconsistencies. Ask pertinent follow up questions. Even in the face of this, some people will attempt to deflect by being deceptive, elusive, and evasive. Don't be fooled by this.

The much practiced rule is to admit nothing, deny everything, and make counter arguments or accusations. This cannot be seen practiced any clearer than during Congressional hearings on capitol hill. Even with the threat of perjury looming over their heads, many who sit across from various Senate and House committees cling tightly to their stories even when it is known they are being less than truthful. What can account for this unwaverability?

Like what was mentioned previously, it isn't

what others know, it's what others can prove. Some understand this more than others. Some things are a matter of someone's word against another's. To some that is a best case scenario that they can live with. Next is being questioned in the face of circumstantial evidence. Which to some can mean or be interpreted as one thing or another. Facing this is also palatable. Least best is when confronted with overwhelming evidence of guilt, association, or lying. Even then, especially during certain confirmation hearings, national security or executive privilege is cited as refusal to answer certain would-be incriminating questions.

One last note on interrogatories, they do not always involve questions. Interrogators are divided into grades and classes. The exceptionally good ones can read you without opening their mouth. Or you yours. They can read you with their eyes. Through yours. The energy you give off is also telling. And so are your mannerisms. Regular encounters allow others to observe various irregularities or inconsistencies. Be mindful of all of this. Do what is in your power and don't be concerned with the rest.

* **Key Points:**
    a. There are hidden dangers in questions
    b. Deny, deny, deny
    c. Don't allow yourself to be sifted

d. Search for the motive of all questions
e. Learn to question widely
f. Information gained from Interrogations doesn't always require words

Card 24: The Talking Skull

Talk - To deliver or express in speech: Utter. To use (a language) for conversing or communicating: Speak.

* Concept/Objective: Too much talking is never a good thing. If your occupation does not require you to be talkative, then be very scarce with your words. The words we speak give birth to realities. Therefore, choose your words carefully. Remember, what you say can and will be used against you. Speak less.

(Questions)
1. What is the story of the talking skull?
2. Why are silent observations powerful?
3. What is at the root of why people gossip or talk frivolously?

I once heard a story about a hunter who was out in the woods hunting. Who at some point stumbled upon a skull. The skull began to speak to the hunter. Being confused, shocked, and alarmed, the hunter questioned the skull as to its presence in the woods by asking the skull, "how did you get here?" "Talking got me here, "the skull replied.

Still not fully understanding why the skull was in the woods, the hunter is said to have gone to tell the king or ruler at that time that he had found a skull in the woods that speaks. Astonished, the king gathered his best minds to inquire of them if they had any knowledge or insight of such a happening. All of which replied they had never heard of such a thing.

At which point the king ordered the wise men to go with the hunter to investigate the matter. The king also sent some soldiers with them and ordered his soldiers to kill the hunter by cutting his head off if he is found to be lying. Once they reached the skull in the woods, the hunter was happy because this pointed to the truth of what he said he saw. The hunter asked the skull to speak. The skull was silent. The hunter repeatedly made this request for the skull to speak. All to no avail. He kept pleading to the skull because he knew that if the skull did not speak it would me the hunter's death.

Finally, when the skull never spoke, the soldiers carried out their responsibility as ordered by the king and severed the hunters head from his body. It lay next to the skull they had found there. Once the wise men and soldiers left, the skull that had previously been there asked the hunters skull what had brought him there? The hunter in turn said that, "Talking got me here ."

The lesson is simple, too much talking is dangerous. Although seemingly extreme, some situations can produce deadly consequences. Words have an uncanny ability to produce a reality for you that you least expect. One that you are unprepared for.

Silent observations are powerful in that you can mentally mull over what you want without exposing it to the outside world. Everyone doesn't need know what is in your mind. Other people's thoughts can interfere with your own thoughts when you invite them in by speaking or commenting on things openly. You open yourself up to be imposed upon. You must never underestimate the power of your words and how they give people assess to your inner sanctum.

Being wordy has never been the hallmark of a great thinker. He is more reticent. People who talk much, think less. The more time you spend thinking, the less time you have to talk. But when you do talk, let it be about something. Never just for the sake of hearing your own voice. Don't be that vain. And let it be to the right audience. Don't make the mistake in thinking that what you have to say is important to others. Unless it is.

When we speak, no matter what it is, worlds are produced. We speak things into existence. Is it not written that, "In the beginning was the word...", also that that word eventually became, "flesh"? Something that can be seen and touched. Words are real. They produce realities. Whatever you desire, speak it into existence.

Often, many problems or conflicts that some people have can be traced back to something somebody said. Words have this insidious effect. You think something is being said in confidence, but come to find out what you said about someone else gets back to that person. Now a firestorm has been produced. If you don't want anything you say to be repeated to anyone else, don't say it in the first place. No one can repeat something that you never said.

Sometimes friends or even family members have problems with each other and are not on speaking terms. If this ever happens to you, don't make the common mistake of thinking that just because this is the case that it is okay to gossip about that individual to someone else who may be at odds with the same person you are. Because guess what? The two gossipers at some point may fallout with each other. And down the line things get mended with one of the other friends or family members, but not the other. And everything you said gets repeated to the other. The point is, you save yourself a lot of headaches and problems by not gossiping in the first place. Don't be a talking skull.

Some who are not guilty of gossip are still plagued with speaking about things with no significance. Just plain nothing. Frivolous things. But why? You don't value time? You don't value life? Neither of these should be wasted. Let the bulk of what you speak about involve that which will feed the mind of someone else and vice versa. Foolish talk can be more detrimental than detrimental acts. Somehow words have this lingering effect. Also, don't be a garbage dump waste site where people drop off nothing but garbage on you. Think about that. What do you think that will produce in you over time?

People generally gossip and talk frivolously because they have nothing of substance to talk about . So what do you expect them to talk about? Other and nothing. Put substance in your head so substance will come out. Talk about taking care of business.

* Key Points:
   a. Too much talking is not good
   b. Talking gives people assess to your inner sanctum
   c. Words produce entire realities
   d. Gossiping is for the immature
   e. Put substance in your head so substance will come out

Card 25: Minimizing Mistakes

Minimize - To reduce or keep to a minimum.

Mistake - A wrong action or statement proceeding from faulty judgment, inadequate knowledge, or inattention.

*Concept/Objective: Mistakes will be made. There is no getting around that. The key thing is not to make great mistakes. The ones that cause too much damage and take too much time to recover from. Be careful and think before you act.

(Questions)
1. Is it possible to be completely mistake free?
2. What are some of the factors that contribute to mistakes being made?
3. How can you minimize the amount of mistakes you make?

Mistakes come in many different forms, levels, and degrees. Mistakes also have varying effects. Some mistakes are easy to recover from, some mistakes take a lifetime to recover from, and others there is no coming back from. But you will never go through life mistake free. It takes almost a lifetime to even learn how to live. This is why there is so much trial and error connected with life. No one is exempt from making mistakes. So the goal then is to minimize the mistakes that any of us will inevitably make. Whether we are young or old, wise or foolish, male or female, rich or poor, it makes no difference. Everyone is prone to making mistakes.

The decisions we make in life are important. The consequences of bad decisions can change the whole course of our lives forever. Others' lives as well can be affected. It doesn't take a whole boat load of bad decisions, all it takes is one. This may cause you to live a life full of regret, guilt, or even shame, depending on what the mistake was. You'd be surprised to know that many people carry burdens with them all their lives. While others accept the mistake for what it was and move on with relative ease.

We are all susceptible to making foolish mistakes. Senseless mistakes. Ones that have neither rhyme nor reason. What we don't want to do is make costly mistakes. Ones that, like was said earlier, there is no coming back from. Even small mistakes, if you make enough of them, can add up. Once your mind has been affected as such and your spirit has been drained as a result, then you can develop a condition of hopelessness. And once all hope is gone, what else is there? Nothing. Then you are rendered powerless. To be rendered powerless is a crippling position to be in and will take you out of the game of power. Make enough mistakes and this is exactly what will happen.

There are psychological and environmental factors to consider. Have you ever examined why you made a particular mistake? Have you ever made the same mistake over and over again? What do you think accounts for this? Is there such a thing as an honest mistake? Does not having bad intentions divorce us from the effects of making a bad decision? Is there a difference between a mistake and an error? And lastly, can a mistake a person makes define them?

The intelligent thing to do would be to uncover the reason why we made this or that mistake with the hopes of not ever making that mistake again. But when we make repeated mistakes, this is more psychological than anything else. Whenever we are hampered by mental defects, then there is little that can be done about that. For you, if you know someone is mistake prone, then you must take it upon yourself to not place a serious responsibility upon that type of person. The ramifications are just too high.

Honesty and good intentions aside, the law of cause and effect still applies. What you do will always produce an effect. Have you ever had an unpleasant experience from someone who had good intentions? You will notice that it does not matter what the intention was. I won't go into the different levels of intentions. Just know that you are tied to your mistakes irrespective of your intentions. It was said at the beginning of this card that mistakes come in many different forms, levels, and degrees. The motive behind your actions will determine whether it was a mistake or an error. Errors are more deliberate. And no, whatever mistake you made in the past does not define who you are today. We grow and learn from yesterday's mistakes.

Faulty judgements, not being focused, and ignorance are the main factors that contribute to mistakes being made. Being subject to a mistake because of any one of these is serious, just imagine when two or even all three apply to you. Let's touch on just one of these.

Of all the things men should protect themselves from, carelessness is at the top of the list. The devil is in the details. Not paying attention to details is to overlook very significant factors that can come back to hurt you. Impatience and distractions precipitate carelessness. Take your time and look over every aspect of what you are about to engage in. Don't count anything as insignificant if it can hurt you in any way.

Environmentally you can't help but to absorb everything around you. If the environment is dark, you will reflect that darkness. If it is other than that, then you will be affected in that way. You inherit traits and characteristics that flow into your bloodstream and infect you from the inside out. Being around powerful people in powerful environments is important if you want to grow in power.

Lastly, when making decisions, take into account the following: don't make emotional decisions, make sure what you decide to do is necessary, measure everything by what it costs you, and ask yourself, how can any decision you make directly or indirectly negatively impact you.

Answer these questions and you will make more sound decisions and fewer mistakes will be made in the process.

* Key Points:
    a. No one is exempt from making mistakes
    b. Enough small mistakes can equal up to one big mistake
    c. Don't be careless, pay attention to details
    d. Being around powerful people in powerful environments is important if you want to grow in power
    e. Ask yourself the right questions before making decisions

Card 26: Total Domination

Total - Comprising or constituting a whole. Entire. Absolute. Utter. Complete.

Dominate - To rule or control. To exert the supreme determining or guiding influence on or over.

Domination - Supremacy or preeminence over another. Exercising mastery of or ruling power over. Controlling influence.

* Concept/Objective: No matter what arena you are in you should be the dominating factor. Wielding your influence to completely subdue and control. Dominate or be dominated. The choice is yours. Exert your dominance, and rule, supremely.

(Questions)
1. How can you establish your dominance?
2. After dominance, then what?
3. Does having influence have anything to do with being able to dominate? If so, in what way?

"And God blessed them, and God said unto them, be fruitful, and multiply, and replenish the earth, and SUBDUE it; and have DOMINION...". 10

People move according to how they perceive people, places, and things. This is why a certain element in society rule by the force of their minds. Using their mind to effect other minds. Physical force is only a small percentage of everything, and not very lasting. While mental force is a greater percentage of everything, and its effect is lasting. This is why your goal should be to win the hearts and minds of others.

To produce the greatest effect, never rely on physicality, your mind has the power to move things. This is why we spent time discussing the importance of grooming your power, your real power, at every available opportunity in an earlier card. True dominance is the embodiment of raw power. How can you dominate without it? You can't and you won't.

Dominance requires a boldness that is unflinching. This does not necessarily entail violence, but it does not negate it either as a means to an end. What is the end? Total domination. Violent excursions are the weakest expression of power. In power you have the ability to make others acquiesce, capitulate, and submit by the force and power of your mind. Violence is always the last resort.

Being dominant demands a certain kind of staunchness. So exert your dominance in such a way so as to completely awe and overwhelm. To do this you must be good, bad, or ugly. The more adept you are you can be all three. Assume either depending upon what the situation calls for.

Staying clean, getting dirty, or destroying are terms descriptive of and correlate to being good, bad, or ugly. Everything has a time, a place, a reason, and a season. Be good when it calls for it. Sheer divinity enables you to dominate dynastically by being a paragon of civility. Be bad when you have to. Get in the mud and associate with the movers and shakers from every sphere, so that if anything moves you will not only know, but you will have a hand in it. Be ugly as necessity requires you to be. Your lethal audaciousness allows you to erase all remnants of opposition or foes.

Once your dominance has been established, then proceed to take control. Direct. Rule. Be Supreme. Orchestrate things to facilitate your objectives. Your control of a particular arena means that nothing happens except that you partake in it. Meaning you benefit. The root idea underlying total domination is supremacy. How can you dominate without being the best? Once your mind has been developed and has evolved from your continued acquisition of a superior knowledge than you previously operated from, all resistance to you will fall. At this point, no matter who rules, your access to anything will be unrestricted.

Let's look at this idea of supremacy a little more and how it relates to total domination. Most are not built to dominate. Some are but don't know it. The vast majority of people shrink from what it takes to be supreme or the best at something. It is unfortunate that they cheat themselves out of something that is their birthright. It requires great mental strength to develop your inner dominance and bring it to the surface.

This could be why it's lonely at the top. Not many are willing to put the necessary work in to be supreme. In the arena of power, you can't be weak or feeble minded. There is no room for laziness or cowardice. You have to fight against anything or anyone that is in your path from you taking your rightful place.

Dominance and influence go hand in hand. You can't have one without the other. Influence has everything to do with being able to dominate. Your power, should people choose to accept it, makes you influential. If they choose to ignore your power, your influence is of no effect. Your dominance depends on your ability to influence people. Without that key element, you won't be able to control, guide, or direct others. True dominance is influential power. Power is your ability to do. When you are truly dominant you can do what you want, when you want, and it matters not who opposes you.

When you reach this level it is because you understand the dynamics of power so intimately that you don't even have to make power moves anymore. Others will fall in line and relinquish to you all that you deserve, willingly and without you having to ask. Power does not have to be forced. Your bearing exudes to one and all how they shall deal with you. Your presence alone is enough to accomplish this. Power will ooze out of your pores. Everything around you is affected by your presence. This just doesn't happen by chance. Dominance is something that can't be given to you, it something that must earned, over time. Put in the work and watch the fruits of your labor. Everything will work out when you put the work in. Dominate, totally.

* Key Points:
- a. True dominance is the embodiment of raw power
- b. Violent excursions are the weakest expression of power
- c. Dominance is yours, but you have to put the work in to get it
- d. To dominate is your birthright
- e. You can't influence without being dominant
- f. When you are truly dominant, it will be manifest to everyone and you will affect all within your sphere

SECTION THREE

♣

CLUBS

* Commentary III:

There are influences in your life that are both apparent and nonapparent that operate on you in ways that may not always be in your best interest. Your liberties, whether you realize it or not, have been usurped from you microscopically in a systematic way, and dare I say, with malicious intent. People in power have grossly abused their power by using it to maintain their stance while siphoning from you your natural resources which have been bestowed upon you by your Creator. This is undeniable and indefensible.

This has made many impotent and rendered them a perpetual dependent. Worst of all is that the vast majority of peoples are blissfully unaware of their purposefully manufactured weakened state. The effects of which seep out in the subtlest of ways making it virtually impossible to detect and pinpoint its origins. The most alarming thing about this seepage is that it always leads to self-destructive thoughts and behaviors. Allowing the hand that threw the rock in the water to remain far removed from the ripple effect it produced.

One of the most difficult things to do is to see what is not readily obvious. The unaided eye will miss it every time. The next most difficult thing is its acceptance once shown to you. Once the layers are peeled back to expose the inner workings of a real, yet cleverly hidden reality, it can be too much for many people to bear, so they willingly turn a blind eye to that which they know exists, even if this knowing is only instinctual.

Having neither the power nor the will to confront things, they reckon, depending upon their socioeconomic status, that they will be content with their lot in life. The top of this socioeconomic class is the most insulated from most of the stuff that the bottom tier suffer from. Ninety-nine percent of this upper class never concern themselves with those on the bottom. They know or believe that their elevated state is supported by the suffering masses on the bottom, like a pyramid structure. Why interfere with the base upon which their fortune was built?

Then you have those in the middle, who ponder why bother with something that does not affect them directly is the common consensus of this class? Little do they know that no one is fully exempt or untouched by this poison. While those on the bottom rung of society simply resort to scraping and scrapping over the crumbs that unintentionally fall from the master's table. The rest have reached their breaking point and have resolved to reclaim what is rightfully theirs. It is these that will benefit the most from this book.

You are engaged in a process to take control over every facet of your life. This process is long, arduous, and requires your full attention. You have to involve yourself completely by actively participating at every stage. There are no shortcuts, yet there are ways to expedite the process. Some things cannot be given to you in life, they have to be worked for. Father may have, mother may have, but God is most liberal to those who get it on their own. Once you earn what you have, it is yours and cannot be taken from you by anyone. Whereas if someone gives you something, then you can be deprived of it at the mere whim of your benefactor.

Self-awareness is crucial in this process. This means that you have to really take stock of yourself and that which surrounds you. Based upon your intuitive understanding of this present day's power structure and its uses and abuses, can you more accurately gain control over the affairs of your own life rather than continuing to relinquish it in the hands of others. This can only happen when you have a general understanding of the controlling influences in your life by governmental means that make you vulnerable to unseen dangers that have and continue to adversely affect your life. The knowledge in this book is designed to help you from being unduly influenced in ways you have no control over.

(Master Strokes)

Cards 27 - 39:

27. Remote Control; 28, Achilles Heel; 29. Ghost Protocol; 30. Handling Enemies; 31. Fighting Fire with Fire; 32..Winning at all Costs; 33. Situational Adaptation; 34. Beachhead Breaching; 35; The Velvet Glove; 36. The Trojan Horse; 37. Fools Rush in Where Wise Men Fear to Tread; 38. The Science of Willing; 39. The Thirteenth Chapter

Card 27: Remote Control

Remote - Separated by an interval or space greater than usual. Far removed in space, time, or relation. Acting, acted on, or controlled indirectly or from a distance. Out of the way; Secluded.

Control - To exercise directing influence over: Regulate. To have power over: Rule. To guide or manage.

* Concept/Objective: There are times when distance is required to operate. Distance that allows you to stay clear and out of the way. Your ability to manage affairs as if you were present is the secret to your success. Especially if those affairs are ugly deeds that you don't want anyone to see or know about, and especially if those deeds can come back to hurt you in anyway.

(Questions)
1. In what way does the remote control method serve as a protective measure?
2. What tools do you need to be effective controlling matters from a distance?
3. Are there occasions when you must cast remoteness aside to do the work yourself?

This card on remote control is self-explanatory, in a sense. So, what we will present here is merely a reminder of sorts of what you should already know and be practicing. The most premier move you can make is to accomplish certain deeds as if you were physically present yourself. Wherever the action happens, if it can have any negative blowback on you, then you don't want to be anywhere around. If there is even the slightest chance of harm, exposure, or loss; then place yourself at the appropriate distance; which is far away from things when they happen.

Assuming you are involved in a highly delicate matter and if your involvement is discovered, and it could cost you in ways that are too much for you to pay or handle, you must remotely control the matter. So you operate and control things through others and or through different channels. The idea is not only to throw people off the scent so you won't be detected, but you don't even want to be suspected. The reasons surrounding why distance is required are many. Aside from basic security concerns, this method is more preferred under ideal circumstances because it gives you a lot of latitude, maneuverability, and deniability.

The other aspect of remote control is practiced less and is often missed due to perhaps emotionalism. I'm referring to the time factor. Time creates distance too. The amount of time that passes between a particular incident and a corresponding response, depending on what it is, can come right back to you. So it is a good practice to exercise patience and wait for the right time to act. Move too sudden and the finger will point right back at you.

If immediacy is not necessary, then it is necessary that you don't respond immediately.

When the dust settles, you don't want to be anywhere around. To protect yourself from all the debris, you need to be protected. Using the remote control method in certain affairs is the surest means of remaining safe. Although you can benefit the most by being in the middle of the action sometimes, if it puts you in harm's way, even momentarily, then you must disengage yourself from that act. Direct involvement, although it can be more beneficial temporarily, must give way to more indirect means that are even more beneficial. You benefit more in the long run, and you are safer than you would be by being too close to unfavorable deeds.

The most effective tool you will need to control matters remotely is a comprehensive knowledge of every aspect of the situation or matter at hand. Next is to have highly competent and trustworthy people to perform much needed tasks. Be careful who you have perform certain tasks because their close ties to you can expose you. I know it is more comfortable to use people we are familiar with, generally this is the best people to use, but don't oblige if it is not completely suitable to do so. This is okay if their involvement will keep your role in the matter hidden. But once it is determined otherwise, then it is best to use someone else, a third party with no direct connection or ties to you.

Having a keen understanding of every aspect of the matter at hand will help you in deciding whether distance, time, or relation alone is necessary to use. You may have to combinate any two or all three components as your assessment of the matter dictates. You would be hard pressed to use anyone of lesser qualities. Do this only if there is no other recourse and the act is absolutely necessary. If it is not necessary, and seeing how what you have to work with is less than optimal, wait, or do it yourself.

Experience will inform you whether or not to utilize the remote control method of operation. As time goes on, the older you get, and the more things can cost you, makes this method the best and more viable option available. Otherwise, don't associate or involve yourself in matters that you can't afford to be in. Again, you instinctively know this, but sometimes we don't respond well to instinctual signals. Don't let any gain or benefit cause you to ignore your best course of action, your safest course of action: remoteness.

The unequaled excellence you strive for depends on you getting the little things right, every time. This is why, although each card has its own distinctive qualities, they are all connected in some way. And each one enhances the other. This particular card embodies the principle of the hidden hand like no other. However, your success herein is contingent upon how successful you are in the various other aspects of power.

The remote control method is the ultimate way of keeping your hands clean and your identity unknown. So one of your greatest weapons happens to be becoming invisible. All you have to do is resist the temptation to want to be in the spotlight or the desire to be the center of attention. Do this and you have mastered another component of power that you can put in your arsenal. And after a while, the deck will soon be stacked in your favor.

The idea for the remote control method of dictating affairs from a distance is not only drawn from the much used device, the remote control, that is used to control your TV, but a multitude of items and things nowadays. Remote controls are designed for convenience, comfortability, and safety that saves you time, energy, and protects you. Ideally, this is the ease with which you should be able to control matters, conveniently, comfortably, and safely while saving time, energy, and limiting dangerous situations, all while at a distance. Things should be as easy as pushing a button.

The director's chair is another example of being away direct involvement in the midst of the action, yet you control all the action. Everything is orchestrated by you, the director. Everything happens as you see fit. You have the ability to move people any way you desire to fulfill the vision in your mind.

Everyone is subjected to your will. This is unadulterated power. To get others to do what you want, when you want, and how you want, by bending them to your will, is one of the goals of power. Be the director by using the remote control method.

So if you want to save time and energy, avoid unnecessary and avoidable harm, or limit or escape unwanted exposure, then the remote control method is the best and only option for you and you should make it a part of your modus operandi.

* Key Points:
    a. If there is even the slightest chance of harm, exposure, or loss; create the necessary distance away from the action
    b. Remotely control matters if your direct involvement could cost you more than you can pay or handle
    c. The passage of time is another way to create distance, use it when applicable
    d. Be aware of who you have perform certain tasks, because their close relationship with you could possibly expose you
    e. Don't let any gain or benefit cause you to ignore your best course of action, your safest course of action, remoteness
    f. The remote control method is the ultimate way of keeping your hands clean and your identity unknown

Card 28: Achilles Heel

Achilles Heel - A vulnerable point.

Achilles Heel - 'When the hero Achilles was an infant, his sea-nymph mother dipped him into the river Styx to make him immortal. But since she held him by one heel, this spot did not touch the water and so remained mortal and vulnerable, and it was here that Achilles was mortally wounded.'   15

* Concept/Objective: Everyone has weaknesses. Something that can be used against them. This goes the same for you too. You have an Achilles, a chink in your castle wall, a soft spot. Whatever your weaknesses are, you should be the first to discover them. Overcome them. Otherwise they will be used against you.

(Questions)

1. Why must any weakness you have be of concern to you?
2. What is it about weaknesses that makes them repulsive?
3. In what way can a weakness be turned into a strength?

Weaknesses, although we all have them, must first be discovered by you. That way you can deal with it. This has two fronts: one, either turn your weaknesses into strengths, or; two, compensate for them in such a way so as to render them unnoticeable and harmless. Weaknesses can be exploited.

They almost always are. This vulnerability keeps you at risk of those who prey on other people's weaknesses. Weaknesses to men are like soft spots are to newborns. They are great points of vulnerability that can irreparably harm you.

No greater arena than that of politics can you find this played out the most when it comes to exploiting weaknesses. Political rivals look for any advantage to win by discrediting and attacking their opponents. This is why smear campaigns are so prevalent in politics. This can range from highlighting past votes that contradict presently held positions, bringing up a past or present scandal, connecting their opponents to unfavorable people that the public has been made to dislike, or even strategically exploiting an emotional weakness that can be used against them. Such as being easily angered or playing to the other's ego. For some political assassins nothing is off limits to them if it will help them to secure some votes.

Weakness is a stench. However, in the nostrils of predators there is no sweeter scent to them. When the scent of your weakness is detected by the nostrils of the wrong type of person, behold and beware. This type of person loves to capitalize on any weakness they can detect in others. When you operate from a position of weakness, you will always be on defense. Strength is offensive. Just like in the sports world, a better offense is always better than the best defense. In other words, you will never be able to win when you don't overcome your own weaknesses. Weakness and victory are two incongruent terms, they have never been synonymous.

Some people parasitically climb their way to the top by not only currying favor from those in positions of power to help them, but they also unscrupulously live off anyone that will allow them to. Human predators are everywhere looking for someone to prey on. They do this because they can. The weak give off a beacon that the strong are drawn to in droves

Whether they have the ability or the imagination to get to the top on their own instead of being a bloodsucker is of no concern to them. Bloodsuckers practice winning at all costs to new extremes and have no qualms whatsoever about it. They wait for others to get and then they do everything in their power to deprive what another has worked hard for. Hyenas do it. Vultures do it. But why? It is in their nature to do so. The world is full of hyenas and vulturelike people so you shouldn't expect them to do anything other than what hyenas and vultures do.

Weakness only begets more weakness. That is the only thing you will ever get from weakness is more weakness. Weak thoughts plus weak actions equals weak results. Strength begets more strength. This too is multiplied and increases as you get more of it. Each one, weakness and strength, can only produce more of itself. I know earlier we mentioned that any weakness you have must be turned into a strength as a way of dealing with it. Since we know that weakness begets more weakness, not strength, then by destroying weakness, you manifest its opposite, strength.

This does not preclude the fact that some people's weaknesses are really their strength. While another's strength can be their weakness. In the case of the former, someone who is overly kind can be run over by the unkind. But this same person's kindness will enable them to enter certain circles and have certain opportunities made available to them that are closed off to a person who is unkind. Then you have someone whose strength is loyalty, but loyal to a fault has its plusses and minuses and can either benefit or harm you.

Overall, weaknesses are not good. Yet, some weaknesses, just like some strengths, is all a matter of perspective and how it benefits the beholder of either. Anything, no matter what it is, can be weaponized and used against you like we described above.

Never, under any circumstances, let anyone know what gets to you. No matter how much they do, don't show it. Once they know your Achilles Heel, then it will be used against you. You too can discover another's vulnerable points and use that knowledge as leverage under the right conditions. As the saying goes, only the strong survive.

* Key Points:
    a. Any weakness that you have must first be discovered by you and dealt with accordingly
    b. Weaknesses can be exploited, and they almost always are
    c. Weakness and victory are two incongruent terms, they have never been synonymous
    d. Predators love and are attracted to the sweet smell of weakness
    e. Weakness begets more weakness, and strength begets more strength
    f. Anything, no matter what it is, can be weaponized and used against you; a weakness or a strength

Card 29: Ghost Protocol

Ghost - A faint shadowy trace. To move silently like a ghost

Protocol - A code prescribing strict adherence to correct etiquette and precedence.

* Concept/Objective: It is good under certain circumstances, to be known, seen, or heard; and it is advisable under other circumstances not to be known, seen, or heard. The specifics of the occasion will guide you. It's a game of hide and seek and roots and shoots. Choose wisely.

(Questions)
1. In the context of this particular card, what is considered the best reputation and why?
2. What makes one invincible?
3. When should the ghost protocol be put into play?

"Formlessness means being so subtle and secret that no one can spy on you. Soundlessness means being so mysteriously swift that no one notices you."[1]

The best reputation is no reputation. What is it about people that makes them want to be seen and known by all? Esteem purposes? A need for validation? Ego? Whatever the case, either confront it and deal with it or expose yourself to the elements at the wrong time and suffer as a result. Allow me to acquaint you with an old tale about three doctors who we'll say are brothers and it was argued of which brother was most skilled at his profession. The one who was known by all, the one who was known by a few or the one who was hardly known at all?

The first brother had a reputation that spanned the entire land and his name was known by all because he was able to perform all kinds of medical feats that remedied all sorts of medical conditions that were in there advanced stages.

The second brother was able to catch whatever ailment a patient had or was suffering from at an earlier stage so his name did not span the entire land but it reached quite far.

The last brother was able to diagnose and medically treat ailments before they barely even had a chance to take form, so his name was barely known at all.

The question was then asked of which brother was the best and most skilled at his craft? The first brother was good, the second brother was better, but the last brother was the best; although he didn't have the reputation his two brothers had.

In the above story, the bigger the reputation, or the more you are known for something does not make you the best or most skilled at that thing. An elite practitioner understands the very nuances of his craft so intimately well that it gives him a mastery that is second to none, no matter what his occupation is.

In the case of the doctor brothers, the third brother was so exceptionally skilled in the art of diagnosis and treatment that there were hardly any occasions where his skill had to be put on display for all to see. The way he treated his patients made them oblivious to the depth of his knowledge, skill, and mastery. By virtue of the advanced medical stages of the patients of the first brother, which was noticeable by all; it was not difficult or surprising to learn that his name and reputation spread far and wide.

It is hard to measure greatness in the reverse context except by extraordinarily gifted minds. And this is why the truly great ones are often unrecognized and underappreciated. Their greatness is enjoyed mostly by themselves. Sometimes they are the only one in the audience witnessing their greatness. It's no wonder that this level of skill and mastery is missed by the average person. Don't take this out of context. The best singers, actors, sports professionals, and the like, are exceptions when it comes to visible and known greatness. Their talent and skill are meant to be displayed, and if you are not of this class, then yours isn't.

Take the issue of conflict for example, when someone has to always deal with conflict by force, and they succeed at removing that conflict, and this is done repeatedly, this person will develop a reputation of being very capable whenever conflict arises to handle it in said manner. Another is able to prevent conflict from escalating to the point where force is necessary. He deals with conflict by way of conciliatory means. He never develops the reputation of forcefulness, but he is still known by how he effectuates peace. Then you have the one who understands conflict so well that he knows how to prevent conflict from arising in the first place? Without the presence of conflict, others are unable to measure his capabilities in dealing with conflict, so he is virtually unknown in that regard.

But I ask you, who was more skilled in dealing with conflict? I think the point has been made.

Pertaining to the matter of invincibility, you are the only one who can make yourself invincible. You control this. No one else does. When you make yourself vulnerable in any sense, then you can be assailed against. Your invincibility lies in your invisibility. This falls under the gambit of formlessness. Making yourself visible is reserved for the rarest of occasions, and then, only if it is beneficial to do so. You must consider the serious and delicate nature of certain affairs. Your exposure, on any level, when it is not warranted, is counterproductive. The spotlight is dangerous except for being on stage. This should not be difficult to understand. Visibility makes you a target. You become predictable. Anything that is visible or predictable is vulnerable and susceptible to outside threats. See card eight.

There are times when you need to just disappear. Get away. You could even hide in plain sight. The bottom line is to become scarce. Withdraw yourself for a while. Conditions are such that your absence is required. You have to know when to withdraw from the scene and go off the grid. How long is determined by the overall circumstances. Cutting the world off is not easy for some of us. You have to be disciplined, comfortable being alone, and above all you need to know when the coast is clear.

The Master's Deck

Surprisingly, depending on who you are, especially if you have developed a certain reputation, the coast will never be completely clear. You will always carry a cloud around you no matter how hard you try to evade attention. Yes, you never want to stick out like a sore thumb under any circumstance unless those circumstances are tightly controlled by you. But always remember, the only nail that gets hammered in is the one that sticks out. Stay flush like all the other nails and you have nothing to worry about.

There are times when your disappearance and unknowableness can work against you. Imagine a sun that never shines? Any extended withdrawal from you, aside from weighing the situation out for clear and present dangers, is not good. The only time the Ghost Protocol is really effective is for security purposes. Even if there are no pressing dangers, you still want to make it a regular practice to move in a way where you are seen but not seen. Heard but not heard. You want others to only be able to faintly detect an outline of you, like a ghost.

Ghost protocol is one of the most elite master strokes and should be employed perpetually even at the most basic level. This means not putting yourself in a position where you are on someone's radar that you shouldn't be on. Be wise. Be as if you are always being watched and listened to, not from paranoia, but for security purposes.

Often, when others don't see or hear from you in a while, more than likely that is the reason. You will have to resort to unconventional methods to make your presence known. Sometimes others will have to be in your shoes to see things in real time to truly understand.

As with all things, there are grades and classes. Ranging from ghost protocol 1 to ghost protocol 3. Gp1 is the most severe stage and this is when there is complete radio silence. At this stage you can't even move wrong. You have to completely insulate and isolate yourself. To expose yourself to anyone, will indirectly expose them and put them at risk. To prevent that you simply vanish.

Gp2 is the intermediate range and it is used to put yourself and others on high alert to certain possibilities that are likely but you are unsure as to specifics, but you know something is afoot, so in these instances you err on the side of caution and take general cover.

Gp3 is what was referred to earlier as the most basic level. This means that you use ordinary measures not to overly expose yourself when moving. Expose yourself, but only when necessary. Reach out, but only when necessary. Be brief. Vague even. Operate like a ghost.

* **Key Points:**
a. The best reputation is no reputation

b. The best skilled are seldomly known by all
c. Your invincibility lies in your invisibility
d. Sticking out is never a good thing
e. Ghost protocol should be perpetually in effect
f. Use the ghost protocol grading system

Card 30: Handling Enemies

Handle – To deal with in a certain way.

Enemy – Something or someone that is harmful or deadly. A hostile adversarial opponent or force.

* Concept/Objective: Enemies are everywhere. The form of an enemy is many and is never constant. Your ability to effectively handle your opponent is important to be victorious. How you do this is the key. And this is predicated on how well you understand your enemies. Always handle your enemies with care.

(Questions)
1. Is an enemy always an enemy, and is a friend always a friend?
2. Who are the most dangerous enemies you have to protect yourself against?
3. Why are strong enemies necessary in life?

Never be so quick to label someone an enemy; and never be so quick to label someone a friend. These two terms are mutually interchangeable. No one is ever completely or permanently an enemy; and no one is ever completely or permanently a friend. There is no permanency in this universe.

I recall watching an interview on TV a while back in which the former Secretary of State, Henry Kissinger stated in reference to America's enemies; "We don't have any permanent friends and we don't have any permanent enemies, only permanent interests." It has been written that a wise man profits more from his enemies than a fool does from his friends. And that the best way to destroy an enemy, at appropriate times, is to make him your friend. Let your interests be your guide in said regard.

I would venture to say that there are three types of enemies who could be considered the most dangerous. Former friends, unseen enemies, and those who have absolutely nothing to lose. There are more, but I will touch on these for now. Just be mindful that enemies come in all shapes and sizes. And their approach is multidirectional.

"Lord, protect me from my friends; I can take care of my enemies." 2

Friends, that's a big word. When it's good, it can be really good. But when it's bad, it can be really bad. Of all people, who knows you more than your closest friends? Who is more capable of moving against you? No one knows you better. This makes a former friend a very dangerous enemy. Formidable. We already know that we will never fully or completely know anyone. This is why one can be a friend today and an enemy tomorrow. We already know how to prepare for all eventualities. We already are aware of how and why we need to utilize certain security measures. There are any number of reasons that can turn a friend into an enemy. Envy being at the top of the list along with some slight or offense. Handle your friends accordingly and stay alert.

Would it surprise you to know that an enemy can be more honest than a friend? Friends rarely ever speak to you of ugly truths. Enemies can be brutally honest. A friend feels that he has much to lose. He doesn't want to hurt your feelings or say anything that could make the relationship awkward. This is not the case with enemies. In these instances, an enemy is more of a friend to you, and a friend an enemy. This is why it is said that, "when your enemy speaks, never interrupt him."   2

Let your enemies speak, especially an angry one. He will reveal things to you in his barrage of words that can help you deal more effectively with him. By interrupting him you mess his flow up and give him time to think. Time to reconsider what he was going to say. Don't give him that time to second guess himself.

Next are unseen enemies. How can you protect yourself from an enemy you don't even know exists? With this kind of enemy not only do you not know the who, but the when and where as well. If that is not a dangerous dynamic, I don't know what is.

Needless to say, your overall moves should account for anyone being a potential enemy to you. Staying alert at all times to anything and everyone will be your key to surviving the attack of an unseen enemy. This does not mean you are suspicious of everyone, but it does mean that you don't put anything past anyone. We have already discussed in an earlier card that those who are the closest to you are the only ones that can hurt you the most. At least more directly and more immediately.

You too can be a dangerous enemy to others without them knowing so. It is never good to broadcast to your enemy that he is in fact your enemy. What sense does that make? None. You lose more than you gain by doing this. You lose all the initiative. At best you gain temporary satisfaction from speaking your mind, but nothing else. Resist the urge to speak your mind unless it is absolutely necessary.

Lastly, when it comes to your most dangerous enemies, it is the one who has absolutely nothing to lose. Usually when a person's back is against the wall, they are desperate which makes them a very dangerous enemy. Never press others into a corner where they feel they only can resort to extreme violence to save their own life. Desperation is a powerful motivator and fills its possessor with a tremendous amount of energy that can give them an advantage over you.

Most people think that having an enemy is a bad thing. It can be but it does not have to be. It used to be puzzling to me when I learned that if you didn't have an enemy, that you should create one. A worthy opponent tests you and brings out the best in you and keeps you on your toes. This is good friction. And friction is necessary if motion is to be made. Opponents push you and challenge you like no one else can. The only exceptions are for those who are highly self-motivated. For they drive themselves by pure ambition from an unquenchable desire to succeed. This comes from something deep within. Which still signifies overcoming opposing internal forces. Enemies of self from within self.

"For it must be noted, that men must either be caressed or else annihilated; they will revenge themselves for small injuries, but cannot do so for great ones; the injury therefore that we do to a man must be such that we need not fear his vengeance." 7

If an enemy cannot be profited from in some way, or if circumstances are unsuitable for caressing, then annihilation is the only resolve. And this is what makes these last few points so critical when it comes to handling enemies. Because nothing is more dangerous for you than to deal with an enemy anywhere between these two parameters. You need to know and understand that there is no middle ground here. Your two options are: caress or annihilate. There is no third option.

What is meant by middle ground? We touched on it earlier when we discussed how it is never a good thing, in most cases, to speak so freely and loosely to an enemy where you give them a piece of your mind. There may come a time when you feel compelled to express your dislike or hatred to someone. Again, whenever this urge comes up, get rid of it right away. How do you benefit from revealing your disdain to someone other than getting, like we said, some temporary satisfaction? But at what cost? Especially if the other person doesn't know that they have made you their enemy. By remaining unseen and unknown you have all the leverage. If one of the three most dangerous enemies are those that are unseen, this works in your favor too.

This is why we began this entire deck of cards with card one being Uncontrolled Emotions. Keeping your emotions in check is so important to your ability to master a lot of situations. When your emotions are out of control, you are out of control. Emotional responses are never good because they rarely work in your favor. Anger is the emotion that causes us to lose the most control in heated situations and makes us say and do things in the moment that can't be undone.

So, anger is the number one uncontrolled

emotion that prompts us to want to argue and even threaten someone. But as soon as our anger subsides, we are able to look at the situation more clearly, but by then it may be too late. It takes great discipline to be able to think through anger. Until you are able to develop to that point, learn to control your anger. Better yet, as best you can, try limiting putting yourself in situations that you know can or will trigger you.

When it is all said and done, you are your own worst enemy. No matter who or what is against you, they or it won't be able to handle you if you handle you first. Although friends fall within the realm of potential internal enemies. Because they are inside your circle. But like we said, the biggest internal enemy is yourself. It bears repeating, no one on the outside of you will ever be able to deal with you if you deal with you. Do this and you will be unassailable.

Lastly, give every enemy their proper due. No matter how invincible you become or think you are, a determined enemy will find a way to get you even if it is a kamikaze mission. Don't underestimate an enemy's potential and don't overestimate his faults thinking he is incapable of anything. Putting into practice these principles will limit costly mistakes when handling enemies.

* **Key Points:**
    a. In applicable situations, no one is ever completely an enemy or a friend
    b. Former friends, unseen enemies, and those who have absolutely nothing to lose are your most dangerous enemies
    c. If you have no enemies, create one, they will keep you sharp
    d. Enemies are either to be caressed or annihilated, there is no middle ground
    e. Arguing with or threatening an enemy is never a good thing and can be more detrimental to you than anything else
    f. Never overestimate the faults of any man, in doing so, you will make costly mistakes in dealing with an enemy

Card 31: Fighting Fire With Fire

Fight - To contend in battle or physical combat. To strive to overcome. To struggle to endure or surmount.

Fire - A highly destructive and all-consuming force. A severe trial or ordeal.

* Concept/Objective: You've heard of turning the other cheek. Yes, forgiveness has its place. But at times you must equally match or contend with an opposing force to gain victory over it. In this sense, two wrongs do make a right. Your back was only meant to bend forward, not back-

wards. Give people back what they dish out and watch what happens.

(Questions)
1. What is meant by fighting fire with fire?
2. What are the laws of retaliation?
3. Are there any circumstances where other conventional methods are more preferable than fire? And why?

"...When you meet a swordsman, draw your sword: Do not recite poetry to one who is not a poet." [1]

The old adage of not bringing a knife to a gunfight is the cornerstone of this card. At minimum you want to match the force that is being applied against you. Doing this only levels the playing field. Which is okay, but what you really want is a clear and decided advantage. You want to subdue and control with an overwhelming force that cannot be defended or overcome. This means if someone draws one sword, you draw two.

There are times when words have no place in resolving conflict. This goes to show you that a soft answer does not always turn away wrath, it increases it. Kindness can have this reverse effect in the realm of power. You wouldn't think so, but the world that we live in has set the standard for so many things that people adopt unquestionably.

Sadly, kindness is synonymous with weakness. Strength must always be displayed. In a world like this you have to be selectively kind, and selectively cruel. Give each man what he is deserving of.

There is a law, whether it is known or unknown; seen or unseen, that governs everything in existence. Nothing is left unregulated. This is equally true when it comes to retaliation. The law of retaliation says that you are never wrong for returning like for like. Whatever has been done to you, you are well within your rights to respond in kind. "And if any mischief follow, then thou shalt give life for life. Eye for eye, tooth for tooth, hand for hand, foot for foot. Burning for burning." 10. This is fighting with fire.

You are even given leeway to lessen the fullest extent of your response at times when appropriate. Never let the law of necessity escape your mind, and how when you do harm to any man it must be done in such a way that you don't have to constantly look over your shoulder for him to take his revenge. This is mentioned to highlight the third and more final option, that of total annihilation. Weigh all of the factors involved to determine which response you choose. An equal force, a lesser force, or a greater force.

Each of these have their own specific dynamics attached to them. Notwithstanding the basic premise of fighting fire with fire to vanquish another, there is a spiritual component to this as well. The goal is ultimately, no matter what force you choose to come from, the main objective is to fix the problem or meet the opposing force perfectly eliminating any adverse drawbacks. And this is the key, 'perfectly eliminating any adverse drawbacks'. This leads us to our next point.

As far as other methods and why they may be more preferable than matching exactly what has been done to you, there is one main reason that needs to be considered. The pendulum, once it swings in one direction, is bound to come back. This represents the law of justice. Anytime we exceed certain limits, this excess has to go somewhere, and guess where it goes? Towards you like the backward swing of the pendulum. The wise know how to get out of the way or sidestep the pendulum when it swings back so they don't get hit with the brunt of what their actions have produced. At least not directly.

Some things, once done, cannot be undone. Be sure when you pull the trigger on your actions that you are sure that is what you want to do. There is no coming back from finality or once something has been put in motion. When I mention the three categorical responses, you are being provided with options that you can have at your disposal.

The least force, if used, must not in any way whatsoever put you in a position to be victimized. Matching your response equally must not put you, at any point, at a disadvantage. The greater force, if used, must not be excessive where the equal force response would have served the purpose just as well. Whatever works best will dictate for you what the best approach is.

Your goal is to not be powerless in any situation. Remember, you want to be able to master any living situation you find yourself in. Mastery here involves the aftereffects as well. What good would it be to overcome at one stage, only to suffer disproportionately at later ones. Don't ignore universal laws at play here. How you retaliate matters. In the end, use whatever force is necessary to win, nothing more, and definitely nothing less.

"Rulers should not go to war in anger, commanders should not battle out of wrath. Act when it is useful, otherwise, do not. Anger can switch back to joy, wrath can switch back to delight, but a ruined country cannot be restored and the dead cannot be revived. Therefore intelligent rulers are prudent in these matters and good commanders are alert to these facts."[1]

* **Key Points:**
    a. Never bring a knife to a gun fight
    b. There are times when words are incapable of resolving conflict
    c. Nothing is unregulated in this universe, all is subject to a law, even the law of retaliation

d. Returning like for like is the basis of the law of retaliation, with varying aspects to it as well
   e. Some things, once done, cannot be undone
   f. Perfectly eliminate any adverse drawbacks by choosing how to appropriately deal with hostile matters

Card 32: Winning at All Costs

Win - To get possession of by effort or fortune. To obtain by work: Earn. To gain. Victorious.

Cost - To require effort, suffering, or loss. The amount paid for something.

* Concept/Objective: It takes a certain kind of mindset to win at all costs. Your mind must be transformed. Do this and you will never take a real loss. But nothing comes without a price. Pay that price and you will never know defeat.

(Questions)
1. What is the best way to ensure ultimate victory?
2. How can you determine in advance whether you will win or lose in any given situation?
3. What should be studied more, success or failure? And why?

"To have ultimate victory, you must be ruthless." [2]

Can you bypass being merciful, kind, and tenderhearted? If not, then you have lost before you have even begun. To be victorious means you have to be ruthless and concern yourself with nothing but whatever it takes to win. Make the bold move when you have to. Don't hem and haw. Don't hesitate. Don't be sympathetic. Don't let your conscience get in the way. How far are you willing to go to win? If you are not willing to go to the extreme, then you might as well rely on good fortune alone to win.

* Warning: If you are unable to fully embody this mindset then you have to own any losses you take. The world is cold, unforgiving, and does not discriminate when it comes to who it keeps at the bottom and who it catapults to the top. Winning at all costs is the same and is not for the timid, the morally smug, or the faint of heart.

"To win without fighting is best."[1]

The mind of man is one of the greatest untapped resources he has. The wise are well aware of this. And this is why they are always found on the winning side of the equation. Ignorance of your own abilities prevents you from realizing that you don't have to lift a finger to overcome. Being able to calculate and rely on your intellectual abilities alone will allow you to win before you even have to fight. Critical thinking is important. You can never win being a non-thinker. A mental slave is the worst of all. Once your thoughts are set free you open yourself up to a wide array of possibilities to win.

Remember, winning is a state of mind. You have to see yourself the winner before you start anything.

Never accept defeat or have a defeatist mentality. No boxer ever enters the ring thinking he won't win, if he does, he surely won't. Failure is never an option. A winner will always find a way to win.

"The wise win before they fight, while the ignorant fight to win."[1]

Weigh things in advance. You are looking for all the advantages and all the disadvantages. The advantages take care of themselves. They can't hurt you. The disadvantages are the concern. In knowing what the disadvantages are and giving them the attention they rightfully deserve, you win. You are looking for any obstacle, in advance, and removing it at the outset or as they come up.

"The inscrutable win, the obvious lose."[1]

When you are obvious it means you are readable. And when you are readable, others know how to deal with you. But when you are not so easy to figure out, you make others to have to work to know how to find a chink in your armor. This is an aspect of winning that is missed by most, but it is an aspect that will serve you well. So learn the lesson of being inscrutable.

Winning at all costs does not mean that you will never take a loss. But any loss you take, should you take one, is not a loss in the traditional sense. Your moves are governed by the law of necessity Even if you lose you still win because you had to move. You have to play by your own rules. Live life on your own terms. Because when you play by the rules of others, they sit in the director's seat. You have to become the director of your own fate. You have to have your own set of rules you live by. It is in this way that you always win. Don't become a conformist unless it is used as a master maneuver.

You can become so adept at the art of winning that you will be able to manufacture your way to a win in a variety of situations. If you maintain control over a given situation, no matter how it unfolds, you will still come out on top. It's a matter of heads you win; tails you win.

Looking at things primarily from the surface one would probably come to the conclusion that success should be studied more than failure. I would like to somewhat go against the grain of that line of reasoning. Mainly because there is more out there to study when it comes to success, but very little, in comparison, when it comes to failure. True enough, when you study the laws that govern success, and you follow those laws, then you should be guaranteed a seat with the successful.

In addition, generally speaking, when you deal with the positives of a matter, it takes care of the negatives. However, this is not always the case. You can do everything right, but somehow, somewhere along the way something goes wrong. It is from this sense that I say that failure should be studied just as equally as success. Failures are good to study because they give you invaluable insight that can help you maintain your position at the top. Wise people learn from the mistakes of others. Study misfortune.

Another thing to keep in mind is that winning comes by effort or by fortune. In either case, embrace it. Even more so, don't allow any one win to make you drunk. Success has that effect on some people, by letting success go to their head. Stay grounded and don't get bigheaded. The more success you attain, the more on top of your game you should be. Never get too comfortable with your success. The greatest point of vulnerability is when you've declared victory. Why is this the case? Victory for some means that the fight is over. You then have a tendency to relax. In this state of relaxation, it makes you vulnerable. The enemies you made on your way to the top will now take advantage of this opportunity to pounce all over you.

One last caveat, to some, winning is all about how you keep score. What does winning really look like? Sometimes something that looks like winning is really the opposite. Sometimes so-called apparent losses are nothing of the sort. The ultimate end will determine whether you won or lost. Even I experience a lot of small losses and setbacks trying to overcome my present situation, but I never get discouraged because I am certain of victory. I see myself crossing the finish line. You too must see yourself the winner no matter how bleak things may look.

Those on the outside looking in, scores your, what looks like losses to them, all out of proportion. Your score card must read a little differently. And it is your score card that counts the most. Judges who score boxing matches score differently from each other based upon what they see. No one sees you like you, nor will they ever, and you shouldn't expect them to. Never be too concerned about others when you make a conscious tactical decision to step out on a limb. Calculated risks are a big part of winning.

Can you suffer humiliation? Can you weather being misjudged? The process of winning is a painful one. But when you do win, it makes all of it worth it. I now understand what is meant by the 'sweet taste of victory'. After all you had to go through and put up with, to have all of that not matter, must be a good feeling. Winning is a state of mind. Always think like a winner. How could you ever lose thinking like that? You can't and you won't. And after a while, you will develop the Midas touch where everything you touch turns to gold.

* **Key Points:**
 a. Ruthlessness is a part of winning at all costs
 b. Weigh advantages and disadvantages
 c. The inscrutable win, the obvious lose

d. You can never win being a non-thinker
e. Winning comes by effort or by fortune
f. A winner will always find a way to win
g. Winning is all about how you keep score
h. Winning is a state of mind

Card 33: Situational Adaptation

Situation - A critical, trying, or unusual state of affairs. A problem. A position with respect to conditions or circumstances.

Adaptation - Adjustment to environmental conditions. To make fit by modifications according to the situation at hand.

* Concept/Objective: The idea here is to learn what it takes to be able to master any living situation. Things change. Tides turn. Inconsistencies abound. Stability is a foreign concept. Your adaptability is how you navigate through all these variations.

(Questions)
1. What is the key to mastering any living situation?
2. Would you rather be the oak tree or the yielding grass?
3. How should you approach unexpected changes?

"The ability to gain victory by changing and adapting according to opponents is called genius." [1]

Your ability to adapt is the key to mastering any living situation. This is the main tool used by masters of change. It is a temporary posture that allows you to navigate your way through unpleasant, complex, or even dangerous situations. Adapting isn't the same as conforming. Conformation is more of a harder stance than adaptation. Adaptation is when you make temporary adjustments. Conformation is forced and non-volitional. While adaptation is a choice and of your own volition. The former deals with rigidity. The latter deals with flexibility. And this is the key, having flexibility of thought. When you are inflexible because of etched in stone views or hard beliefs, then you strip yourself of the ability to maneuver your way through what you will no doubt be confronted with in life.

Rigidity is a sure means of eventually being broken. You have to know when to bend with the momentum of the moment. When you bend on your own accord, you are in control. When you are forced, the control is another's. Flexibility of thought enables you to contort your thinking to model and match the present situation. This is why there is never any set way of approaching any matter. There is no rule that can be laid down with certainty without an occasion to break from it. Circumstances will always change. This change dictates what you do or don't do. Sounds simple enough doesn't it?

So if I asked you the question on what would you rather be, the oak tree or the yielding grass?

Think about it. Here you have a strong immovable object in the oak tree on one hand, and on the other hand you have grass that yields under the slightest pressure and is tread upon by men. One, the oak tree, is unbending even in the most violent of storms. While the yielding grass is bent every which way with even a gentle breeze. So, again, which would you rather be? The seemingly strong oak, or the seemingly weak grass? Picture this first:

"The grass bends easily in the wind. The great oak stands unmoved. A strong wind can uproot the oak, but no wind, however strong, can uproot the grass that bends flat before it." 5

This gives a clear picture of what is meant by bending with the momentum of the moment. When you are overly rigid or too stiff, you break easily. That's if you take the posture of the oak tree. Whereas if you choose to reflect the yielding grass, you will bend but not break. Even though both are strongly rooted, one bends, the other doesn't. Tactically bending won't uproot you from your core beliefs or values in as much as the bending grass isn't uprooted from the ground even during hurricane force winds.

No matter how much you prepare for certain things in life, sometimes things just don't turn out as planned. Life has an uncanny way of throwing things your way that goes against everything you ever thought, imagined, or expected. This is when you must seek alternative ways to deal with situations that you previously didn't even consider. This is where being able to adapt comes into play based upon the situation at hand.

Your adjustment to environmental conditions means straying from linear thinking or having a one track mind. It is advisable to modify your way of thinking or your usual way of doing things to fit the uniqueness of your present situation. How many times has someone refused to adjust to modern times by holding on to archaic viewpoints or methods? Businesses would not survive if they did this. This is why they are always looking for creative and innovative ways to reflect changing times and conditions.

Militarily speaking, preplanned missions may have to be tweaked in the field of operation to adapt to changing conditions as they arise, otherwise the troops may not make it out alive. Every situation may not contain this level of severity, nevertheless, if you are not open to different ways of dealing with matters, although it might not be a matter of life or death, it could possibly mean the difference between success or failure.

Change is the only constant thing in this universe. Because of the ever changing landscape that time brings, you should expect change as a natural course of things. By expecting the unexpected, you expect everything. There should be no situation that you are unable to adapt to. Sometimes you won't have a lot of time to adjust, your ability to adapt may at times have to be instantaneous.

Everything changes, people too. Change, no matter how slight, especially when it comes to people you deal with, should cause you to mentally position yourself to match that change. This entails so much. Think in terms of security and you will be just fine. If you don't properly adapt yourself according to the situation at hand, then you will potentially suffer as a result.

* Key Points:
- a. Your ability to adapt is the key to mastering any living situation
- b. Adapting is not the same as conforming
- c. Rigidity is dangerous, become flexible instead
- d. There is never any one set way of doing anything, rules must be bent accordingly
- e. Modify your way of thinking or your usual way of doing things to fit the uniqueness of your present situation
- f. By expecting the unexpected, you expect everything

Card 34: Beachhead Breaching

Beachhead - An area on a hostile shore occupied to secure further landing of troops or supplies. A foothold. A point to be advanced from.

Breach - A broken, ruptured, or torn condition or area. A gap.

* Concept/Objective: Most people have walls up. People are naturally resistant when they don't know you, and even some that do know you. There is a way to break these walls down. It takes time and skill to breach. In the end, you want people to lower their resistances to you. This is how you can measure your power and the power of others.

(Questions)
1. What's the science behind establishing beachheads?
2. Can anyone be breached?
3. How can you prevent yourself from being breached?

The term beachhead breaching refers to being able to establish a stronghold in the mind of almost anyone. Where you get others to see you how you want them to and thereby dealing with you in a manner closely resembling how you want them to. All in all you are creating an ally. Someone who does your bidding, knowingly or not. Their mind is the battlefield that you must conquer.

Understanding the science of sight and sound will put you in the best position to establish a beachhead in the mind of almost anyone. Controlling their perception of you is what you are after.

This perception is formed by what they see you do and what they hear you say.

Light travels at the rate of 186,000 miles per second and sound travels at the rate of 1,120 feet per second. And since light travels faster than sound, people will always pay more attention to what they see you do quicker than what they hear you say. The point is that what people hear coming out of your mouth has to match what they see coming from your actions. Although both communicate something about you, visuals have a greater impact and impress that much more. Actions really do speak louder than words.

It bears repeating, when you are able to control what people see when it comes to you, and control what they hear coming from you, then you have the basic ingredients in establishing a beachhead. Who can refuse to make a judgement or form an opinion by what they see? Who can refuse to make a judgement or form an opinion by what they hear? These are the two primary senses that are used to influence another's perception of you.

Now, you may be of those who could care less how you are viewed by others. You could even be one who may have a need that not just anyone can meet. Okay, if that is the case, then so be it. If it is, then you should never complain about your inability to have mastery over any particular matter involving those whom you so carelessly disregarded.

However, in being so nonchalant about that, you forfeit your right to have control over a very important facet of your life. The I don't give a damn mentality will never serve you well. If you are already established and your position is secure, then this applies less to you than someone who is trying to climb their way to the top.

Most anyone can be breached. Some are more difficult than others to get through to. All it takes is time and effort. Your tactical and maneuverability skills are what will enable you to establish yourself firmly in the heart and mind of anyone. Everything you do must be tailor made for whoever you are trying to breach. Letting no detail go unattended. And leaving nothing to chance. Always controlling the who, the what, the when, the where, and the how.

This may seem overly technical but you literally have to orchestrate all these different components to be successful in establishing a beachhead. The greater the target is, it will require of you a more advanced skill set. Greatest of which is practicing patience and gaining as much knowledge about the other person as possible. Any premature advancements can destroy all hopes of winning someone over. If this happens, all may not be lost, but you may have to hit the reset button and begin again.

Who you hang around or allow to hang around you is a matter that should not be neglected either. Remember, sight. If you are seen with the wrong person, at the wrong time, then all bets are off, and the wall that was just beginning to lower for you raises back up never to come down again. Why? Their preconceived notion or idea about someone who you surround yourself with that is looked upon in a negative light can have that same negativity transferred to you, even if it is misplaced or undeserving. We are dealing with perceptions and how opinions are formed by them. See card forty-two.

Most of us practice beachhead breaching quite regularly. If you are a man, just think about a woman you want and how you would court and woo her. Or if you are a woman and you have your eyes on some man that you want. How do you go about getting him or her? You control your words when you speak to them, you especially pay attention to how you present yourself from your hair, to your clothes, etc.

In my opinion, the only viable way to protect yourself from being breached would be to always be security minded, which means to stay alert and aware to the motives of others when you are drawn into something or some place by someone. Just as easily as your perception of someone is formulated by seeing and hearing, yours is too of others. Applying the concepts and principles in other cards will assist you in this matter. Namely security measures and battle concept.

* **Key Points:**
   a. Establishing a beachhead is essentially creating an ally
   b. Understanding the science of sight and sound will put you in the best position to establish a beachhead
   c. People's perception of you is determined by what they see of you and what they hear coming from you
   d. Although there are degrees of difficulty, almost anyone can be breached
   e. Everything you do must be tailored to the person you are trying to breach
   f. Practicing patience and gaining as much knowledge about your target are the greatest skills needed in beachhead breaching

Card 35: The Velvet Glove

Velvet - A characteristic of velvet, as smoothness or softness.

Glove - To cover as if with a glove.

* Concept/Objective: Being bold, brash, and uncivil will only carry you so far. What's wrong with being nice or acting kind? Your confidence lies in the fact that just beneath your kind exterior is an iron hand that can crush anyone into smithereens should you have to. Approach situations with a little more tact and you'd be surprised at the results you will get. Coaxing goes a long way.

(Questions)
1. What should your concept of being shrewd be?
2. When should your velvet glove be removed to display your iron hand?
3. What is the difference between hard and soft tactics, and which one is more effective?

Shrewdness is a state of mind that we all should embody; however, it is one that should be brilliantly hidden in the deep recesses of the mind and should be felt more than seen or heard. Shrewdness and its associated actions do not necessarily imply or entail being evil, wicked or immoral. Not at all. It is merely an inner tenaciousness and will to succeed and win no matter the odds, no matter the circumstances, or no matter the difficulties. Being overtly bold or brash should be reserved for its proper place and time. All in all, your mask of civility should remain intact, and your velvet glove on, unless otherwise called for.

With an iron hand inside a velvet glove you can confidently wield your strength in a couched manner. Your velvety actions, should they be misread and or does not accomplish your objectives, then you can always resort to a harder approach. The big difference between you and others is that you act nice because you want to, while others do so because they have to. For you it is purely tactical. Nothing more. It is definitely a shrewd way to move but an effective one. Your goals are the only thing that matters.

This does not take away from the fact that you can and do have very real and genuine relationships where your kindness is not an act at all. This applies in situations where you are either negotiating for something, establishing some form of beachhead, or putting down a power play. Force is what moves people. It doesn't have to be brutish. You have various tactical means at your disposal. Tailor your approach to the specific individual or occasion. Entice. Induce. Lure. Draw in. All of this can be accomplished by the power of your mind. If this fails, then take your glove off, both of them.

This is the only time it is advisable to remove your velvet glove, after you have exhausted every other means to coax someone to succumb to your smooth way of dealing with them. For no other reason should you remove your glove. Until that moment arrives, continue to be kind, for it is like the tip of an arrow that will effortlessly pierce through the heart of anyone it touches. Being cruel in a kind way is nothing more than a tactical way of being shrewd.

In your hand is the hiding of your power. Imagine having an iron hand inside a velvet glove and someone shook your hand, even though they don't feel the iron directly, don't you think they can still feel the hardness of it? Your strength and your power will always be felt no matter how they are displayed.

So, no matter how delicate you handle someone, because of your hidden power, they can feel it beneath the surface. Always hide your power unless its outward expression will serve the purpose far greater. Never parade your power just for the sake of doing it. In doing so, even though strength is being displayed, it signals an internal weakness. Whereas just the opposite is true when you cleverly conceal it. Can't you see the power in that?

The main difference between hard and soft tactics is the ability to use either brute force or being able to finesse a situation. Finessing is more of an art. You may wonder, why does it matter as long as you get the result you want? Don't forget the interloping of various cards and there potential for success or failure. This is done by measuring everything by what it costs you and not experiencing pyrrhic victories. Finessing requires more mental ingenuity. More thought has to be put into a situation. More needs to be considered. As a result, you can achieve your objective more effectively and more securely without any adverse residual effects.

Tyrannical methods are always short lived. And the dissatisfaction they leave in their wake creates all sorts of security risks that are almost always too many to prepare against. This is why wearing a velvet glove to cover your shrewd actions is one of the wisest moves you can make, and the one that yields the greatest results in the long run.

Politeness will carry you much further than rudeness. Remember, always weigh the advantages and the disadvantages. Don't you think it is more advantageous to be courteous and respectful than it is to disregard the feelings, concerns, or wishes of others? Of course it is. The sweetness of your language and your mannerisms you will be to others as honey is to bees. This is why they say you can catch more bees with honey than you can from vinegar. Dip your words in honey and watch as people willingly come to you. The thing to focus on is doing or acting however is necessary and most effective to win. There are limits to this as with anything. That line is yours to draw.

* Key Points:
    a. Shrewdness is a state of mind that should be brilliantly hidden in the deep recesses of your mind
    b. Being overtly bold or brash should be reserved for its proper place and time
    c. A velvet glove allows you to wield your strength in a couched manner
    d. When your soft tactics fail, then take your gloves off, both of them

e. Your kindness is like the tip of an arrow that will effortlessly pierce through the heart of anyone it touches

f. Always hide your power unless its outward expression will serve the purpose far greater

g. Politeness will carry you much further than rudeness

Card 36: The Trojan Horse

Trojan Horse - Someone or something that works from within to weaken or defeat.

* After besieging the walls of Troy for ten years, the Greeks built a huge, hollow wooden horse, secretly filled it with armed warriors, and presented it to the Trojans as a gift for the goddess Athena, and the Trojans took the horse inside the city's walls. That night, the armed Greeks swarmed out and captured and burned the city. A Trojan horse is thus anything that looks innocent but, once accepted, has power to harm or destroy. 15

* *Concept/Objective: The concept of giving before you take is a time tested strategy that is relatively fool proof. Not many are able to turn down a free gift. You can. And you must. Always look for the attached string whenever you are presented with something that you haven't given equal exchange for. Don't blindly reach for the dangling carrot. It is only meant to entice you.*

(Questions)
1. How can the Trojan horse be best used as a tactic?
2. Is there any such thing as 'no strings attached'?
3. What can be considered the best 'Trojan Horse' to use?

Who can resist a gift or something for free? Hardly anyone. If you want to open others up to be invaded, then be a highly selective and generous gift giver. The gift can be an actual gift, it can be a favor, or even a kind word; flattery included. As long as what you are extending is something that is accepted by the other person. Once they accept it and have it in their possession, then it's game over for them.

We all have chinks in our armor of some kind. A way in. No one knows your areas of vulnerability more than you do. Others are always prying and probing for these areas to infiltrate you. These are the areas you have to fortify the most. You cannot afford to be lax when it comes to securing your internal systems. Even though it is not as easy to notice or detect internal threats, you compensate for this difficulty by establishing protocols that are breach proof. Don't compromise any of them for any reason and you won't be compromised.

The importance of this lies in the fact that the trojan horse tactic works both ways. You can use it as an effective offensive strategy, but others can as well. Knowing this, you are able to be conscious of the attempts that others employ to try to enter your circle. Always critically inspect everything and thoroughly investigate anyone who enters this restricted area which is your personal space. If they don't possess the proper credentials, then they must be ousted with extreme prejudice.

Any harm done to you will only be able to develop or originate from within. By keeping your ranks close, you are more likely to prevent these types of endogenous threats. As long as the core of your upper management team, those in leadership positions, or the heads of your organization are tight knitted and they all embody and subscribe to the principles of that team, group, or organization, then you can live with the results.

Rarely ever is there an instance when something is done for you that it is not connected to some form of debt, obligation, or even a trick or deception. There is always a string attached to it in some form or fashion. There are occasions when someone only gets personal satisfaction from doing something good for someone else. This is rare, even in this, something was gained. The point is, no one ever does anything without a motive. And usually that motive works to bring something beneficial or pleasurable to the giver of that gift, the bestower of that favor, or the speaker of that kind word.

The lesson is simple, whatever you want, pay for it. Don't be indebted to anyone. Debt or hidden obligations are dangerous. Whenever you owe someone, and this does not necessarily have to be money, and in most cases it is not, but they will have certain expectations of you. And unmet expectations produce a state of mind in others that can be detrimental to you. Spoken or otherwise. But more often than not, you won't even know about it, which is even more dangerous. Pay your own way as much as humanly possible and none of that will be an issue for you.

Nothing could be more tactfully effective than playing the trojan horse yourself. In the ideal situation of course. You become the gift that keeps on giving, but inside of you contains the means by which others are weakened or destroyed. To be effective as a trojan horse you must become the perfect fulfillment of another's desires or whatever they have an appetite for. Whatever it is they crave or are susceptible to, you must supply it. This means you have to know your targets by the behavioral jackets you have assembled about them. These behavioral jackets are explained more in depth in card thirty-nine.

Other than yourself, women are the best trojan horses there are hands down. They are naturally more suitable to fit the mold of one who is able to seduce and charm their way into anyone's heart and mind. They can gain access to areas that are generally closed off to men. The specifics of the situation will let you know if a man, a woman, a gift, or a favor is the best option to use as a trojan horse. Whatever it is, it has to be the perfect decoy to throw others off your trail.

*** Key Points:**
- a. Although it is hard to resist a gift or something for free, you must in order to keep yourself from being possibly infiltrated
- b. In knowing where your vulnerabilities lie, you know where to place your fortifications
- c. Always critically inspect everything and thoroughly investigate anyone who enters your personal space
- d. Any harm done to you will only be able to develop or originate from within, so keep your ranks close to prevent most endogenous threats
- e. No one ever does anything without a motive, so be very wary of anything that is given to you or done for you
- f. Nothing can be more tactfully effective than playing the trojan horse yourself, other women in those special occasions

Card 37: Fools Rush in Where Wise Men Fear to Tread

Fool - A person lacking in prudence or judgment.

Rush - To move forward, progress, or act with haste or eagerness or without preparation.

Wise - Characterized by wisdom. Marked by deep understanding, keen discernment, and a capacity for sound judgement. Good sense.

Tread - To walk or proceed along.

* Concept/Objective: Take your time before going headfirst into a situation. Slow down. Don't rush. Exercise good judgment and common sense. Slow and steady wins the race. Develop patience and watch how things begin to take shape for you. Tread light, but firm, as you cross the finish line.

(Questions)
1. Is ignorance really bliss?
2. How do you endure the seemingly unendurable?
3. What should be emulated more, the hare or the tortoise?

"For in much wisdom is much grief; and he that increases knowledge increases sorrow."   10

Wisdom of what? Knowledge of what? Wisdom and knowledge about the harsh realities of life? Human conditions? If many knew of the hidden atrocities that exist in the world, it would shock and grieve them tremendously. The true state of affairs is a sad thing, and the more you learn of these affairs, it no doubt would make you grieve and experience sorrow. Not being wise or knowledgeable of these things would spare you the grief and sorrow that come as a result of knowing. In this sense, ignorance is bliss. But this is not what we are after. There is another dimension I want to put forth.

There are two sides to every coin. I figured that there must be another way of looking at this. Ignorance is being without the knowledge of something or someone. I often questioned the much used phrase that, "Ignorance is bliss." I did not see how these two terms, ignorance and bliss, were mutually compatible. I wondered was the person that came up with this phrase, ignorant his or herself? I still wonder. I suppose that if you are at the bottom rung of society, or in some powerless position, and your outlook on your condition is bleak, and you feel that you are helpless to change things, then you would develop an alternative reality that would allow you to cope with that condition. An element in society chooses to remain ignorant for so-called sanity purposes.

I will tell you here and now that there is nothing blissful about being ignorant. Nothing at all. How can you be happy being ignorant? There is no joy in that. Except of course for those who profit off your ignorance. Now, from that perspective I can see how being ignorant is bliss. These people, the profiteers, I would presume, are not of the class of those who are of the ignorant. Their livelihood is sustained by the ignorant. The ignorant, to their own chagrin, keep the knowing ones in a perpetual state of happiness.

No matter how bad things are, they have to run their course. This is no different than the common cold. It has a beginning, a middle, and an ending. All things do. Hard times included. I know that it can feel like the weight of the world is on your shoulders at times, but no man is ever burdened with anything that he does not have the ability to endure. But how do you endure? By enduring, that's how. By developing patience. By not giving in to a particular hardship. Because if you don't endure or develop patience, you may be compelled to do something, anything, to get that burden off of you. In doing so, you can take an already bad situation and make it worse by trying to interrupt a natural process which is never a good thing.

Some things can't be rushed. Wise people know this. Fools, or the ignorant, don't. A wise person can look beyond the present into the future, while a foolish person barely sees what is in front of him. Taking your time has benefits. The race has never been to the swift. Not when it comes to this marathon called life.

In the Aesop fable of the tortoise and the hare,

it is a principled story of a race between a turtle and a rabbit. By any stretch of the imagination, the rabbit should win the race. However, the turtle shows us how slow and steady wins the race. The turtle was calm, patient, and moved according to its own abilities, never veering off course. Not rushing or trying to keep pace with the rabbit. The rabbit, thinking that nothing as slow as a turtle could possibly beat him in a race, prompted him not to take his opponent as serious as he should have so he dillydallied around until it was too late.

By the time he looks up, the turtle was slowly, but surely, crossing the finish line, first, ahead of his much faster opponent. His focus and patience paid off which were guided by wisdom. He knew too, that by all rights the rabbit, under normal circumstances, should have finished the race before him. But he never concerned himself with what the other could do, which he had no control over. His attention was on himself. The rabbit on the other hand was distracted and was all over the place acting foolishly.

Become knowledgeable and wise to the nature of things. They will guide you far greater and carry you much further than ignorance and foolishness can. Grief and sorrow are as natural to human conditions as anything else. So it is better to experience grief and sorrow from knowledge and wisdom than it is to suffer unnecessarily from the lack of either.

Ignorance should be looked at like an enemy, wherever you recognize it in yourself, destroy it by gaining knowledge. Live within yourself like the turtle and don't be impatient when it appears others are advancing faster and further than you. Like the turtle, never be in a rush, and in the end you will get there still. This is a prime example of:

"Leaving after others but arriving before them." 1

* Key Points:
    a. Get knowledge and become wise and never take the position of being ignorant
    b. Ignorance is not bliss, at least not really
    c. You endure by enduring
    e. Patience is more than a virtue, it is a must have
    f. Be the best you that you can be and let others be them

Card 38: The Science of Willing

Science - The state of knowing. Knowledge as distinguished from ignorance or misunderstanding.

Will - The force and power of your being. The faculty of conscious and especially of deliberate action. The power of control that the mind has over its actions.

Willing - An active process of producing what you desire. Bringing into fruition or manifesting what is in your mind.

Concept/Objective: Everything that you see came from something that you do not see. The mind of man is the vehicle by which worlds are built. You have the power and ability to envision and to cast that vision down the corridors of time as it unfolds right before his eyes. Exercise it.

(Questions)
1. Why is an indomitable will needed in times or cycles of crisis?
2. What kind of mind must you have in order to will things into existence to the extent that you can dictate what your future yields for you?
3. By what means, method, or process can you will things into existence unerringly?

A weak will is the primary cause of your inability to successfully cope with the problems of life. A weak will is responsible for you not being able to will things into existence. You have within you a power directly from The Creator that you are imbued with. A power that has the potential to reach unimaginable heights and achieve unlimited results. There is an element in society that continuously suffers because of having a weak will, an underdeveloped will. The will, the force and power of your being, needs to be developed. But how? With what? Trials and Resistance. Facing the former and overcoming the latter.

Trials help build your will because they provide the necessary resistance that strengthens your will. Trials are a natural part of life. When they come, and they will, it is better to withstand and endure rather than to fold or succumb. If you don't do this, withstand and endure, then your will will be reduced to the point that it resembles a fallen leaf on a windy day. Whichever way the wind blows, so will you.

You have been made powerless to resist the force of the trial so you are pushed and pulled every which way. If you want to conquer and not be conquered; then learn to build your will by overcoming resistance. This means you have to deal with things head on. Running away every time something unpleasant or difficult comes up only weakens your will instead of strengthening it.

Willing things into existence is predicated upon having a strong will. An indomitable will. Now you have to grow into a mind that is fully equipped to bring in a reality of your own choosing. What type of mind is that becomes the question? The very Mind of God Himself. Jesus had this mind and was tasked with the responsibility of ushering in an entire world. How could this happen unless he had the creative faculties necessary to accomplish such a seemingly tall order? All we're after here is ushering in our own tiny world within the macrocosmic world. God's creation, and how He willed things into existence is the template that needs to be used to duplicate the same process.

Once your will has been strengthened, and your mind has evolved, the only thing next is to start willing. It all starts in your mind. Meaning you have to be able to visualize what you desire. Absent this, the process is halted immediately. You need a strong desire. Without this, the process can't even begin. You have to organize things and people in your life in such a way to help facilitate the manifestation of what you desire. Good planning coupled with long-range vision is needed to have pinpoint accuracy so that you hit your mark every time.

Understanding the law of cause and effect is one of the most important features of willing. Causes produce effects. Effects then become causes that produce other effects. This cycle continues and is unending. The best way to control the effect is to be able to control the cause that produces it. In controlling causes, you are exerting mastery over circumstances. Exerting mastery over circumstances means you are dictating what is produced. To do this you must have an intimate knowledge of the nature of things. Without this knowledge, your ability to master anything is hampered. When you get to this point you then can unerringly bring about what you desire with mathematical precision.

In this process alone, the science of willing, it should be noted how many of the cards in this book are interrelated and have a direct bearing on one another. For instance, when it comes to the science of willing, you will need great control over your emotions, know how to plan in secret, develop your inner power, and be able to withstand pain, adversity, and setbacks. So these cards; uncontrolled emotions, hidden plans, personal grooming habits, adversarial companionship, and so many others, are indispensable. It will not bode you well to isolate any one card without bringing to bear whichever other card is necessary to enhance the fullness of another.

Lastly, because of the difficulties attached to bringing forth into reality what is in your mind, you must be determined. Ever so determined. This means that your mind is made up and you have decided that nothing will interfere with you making manifest what you desire. When you can say this to yourself, and mean it, nothing will prevent you from manifesting what you desire. This is why developing your will is the key. Where there is no will, there is no way; but where there is a will, there will always be a way. Start Willing.

* **Key Points:**
    a. A weak and underdeveloped will is responsible for you not being able to will things into existence
    b. Trials and resistance help build your will

c. Growing into the Mind of God is a prerequisite to being able to will things into existence
d. Understanding the law of cause and effect is one of the most important features of willing
e. Where there is no will, there is no way; where there is a will, there will always be a way

Card 39: The Thirteenth Chapter

Spy - One who keeps secret watch on a person or thing to obtain information. To observe or look for something: Look. To watch secretly usually for hostile purposes.

Intelligence - Information concerning an enemy or possible enemy; an agency engaged in obtaining such information. Any information involving a person, a group, or a place of interest.

* Concept/Objective: You can't be everywhere all the time. Besides, you only have one pair of eyes. Find ways to spy on others of your choosing. Arm yourself with this foreknowledge, and it will give you a leverage that is second to none. Don't, and your mastery and control over future outcomes will be greatly impeded.

(Questions)
1. How valuable is espionage? And why?
2. In what way does intelligence differ from mere information?
3. How can you protect yourself from the prying eyes of others?

Note: The Art of War by Sun Tzu is comprised of thirteen chapters; the thirteenth of which is entitled, "On the Use of Spies". Therefore, knowing that I wanted to make this subject, spying, a card, I simply referred to it as the thirteenth chapter. Hence, the title of this card.

"So what enables intelligent rulers and good commanders to move in such a way as to overcome others and accomplish extraordinary achievements is advanced knowledge. Advanced knowledge cannot be obtained from supernatural beings, cannot be had by analogy, and cannot be found out by calculation, it must be obtained from people..." [1]

By virtue of the various and broad ranging intelligence gathering agencies in America, not to mention around the world, this alone tells us how much importance and value is placed on having a storehouse of intelligence. Whether all the gathered intelligence will ever be used is another story. Intelligence is graded according to its value and usability. Nevertheless, to have and not need is better than to need and not have when it comes to Intel.

Most important is knowing about your rivals. Where is this knowledge going to come from? Is it going to be volunteered to you from them? I beg to differ. Is it going to fall out the sky? Absolutely not. Your ability to influence future events is predicated on the Intel you have on others. Without it you cannot effectively rule. Spying is your very own crystal ball. It enables you to see into the future. and control future outcomes.

The main thing you are after is knowledge about someone else. Their character, where their loyalties lie, their abilities, their plans, their weak spots, and so on. You do this by developing behavioral jackets. Which is nothing more than a portfolio of information that you gather that highlights someone's strengths, their weaknesses, their habits and vices, their friends and foes and other associates. It can also reveal their motives, desires, and hopes and aspirations.

People simply won't just freely give you this type of information, you have to spy, by monitoring or by probing, indirectly of course. You could use others whom you trust to provide you with gathering this information. This is only safe if they are competent enough and they are more loyal to you than they are to the target they are spying on. The last thing you want is for someone to tip your hand. You are most qualified to gather this Intel, and whenever the opportunity presents itself, rely on your own abilities or your most trusted friends.

"Rulers see through spies, as cows see through smell, Brahmins through scriptures and the rest of the people through their normal eyes." 2

The difference between intelligence and mere information is how it is gathered and what it is used for. Both are information. One, intelligence, is used to describe a very specific kind of information. The kind of information you need to get a handle of things and that allows you to control situations in unknown yet effective ways. Why leave things exclusively in the hands of others? Why rely on chance? You control the odds when you have foreknowledge about a matter that others don't have.

Look no further than insider trading and how this advance knowledge is used to benefit the knowing to the detriment of the unknowing. Knowledge is power, and is not this the goal you are after? Of course it is. There is a bonus to all of this, when you are able to masterfully circumvent things and dictate future events, you will create an enviable myth like reality around you because of this ability. Don't underestimate how powerful it is to know what others don't know. It puts and keeps you in the driver's seat

In today's world it is virtually impossible not to be spied on. With all of the advancements in technology and the sophisticated ways in which it is used makes spying on anyone, anywhere, relatively easy. Notwithstanding, there are basic, conventional steps anyone can take to limit what is spied on and how much. Especially by way of electronic means because people leave their electronic fingerprints everywhere that can be used to track their activities.

Now, it all depends on what aspect of information about yourself you want kept from others. Just don't leave any trails that can be followed, or at least limit them and you'll be okay. When it comes to in person spying, don't allow yourself to be sifted or probed. If you do allow it, then provide false or misleading information.

* **Key Points:**
   a. Having a storehouse of intelligence is important, it is better to have it and not need it, than it is to need it and not have it
   b. Spying is your very own crystal ball, it enables you to see into the future
   c. You can use others, but you are most qualified to gather the necessary Intel you are after
   d. The main difference between intelligence and mere information is how it is gathered and what it is used for
   e. You control the odds when you have foreknowledge about a matter that another does not have
   f. It is impossible not to be spied on, but there are basic precautions you can take to minimize what and how much others know.

SECTION FOUR

♦

DIAMONDS

* Commentary IV:

Other people are always trying to get you to see things their way. To do things their way. All under the guise of good advice. Good advice is good, but only if you value it. Good advice has two parts to it. Half of good advice is only good if you take it. The other half is good only if it works. This means you must recognize it when it is offered, and you must be wise enough to use it when you have it. This discernment is predicated upon what you think right and wrong is.

Sometimes something can be right for someone else but wrong for you. Or wrong for someone else but right for you. I think we have all been there where everybody else knows what is right for us but us. Not saying that what was offered was not or is not right. But ultimately, right and wrong has to be determined by you. And there is a way to come to this determination.

So, how do you determine the rightness or wrongness of a thing? Well, aside from the previous point, I once came across something that said, if I recall correctly, that right and wrong is situational. In the right situation, nothing is wrong. And in the wrong situation, nothing is right. It took me some time to get it, but I concur completely. A popularly held view of a thing does not determine whether it being right or true. Conversely, just because something is unpopular does not make it wrong or untrue.

Some people buy easily into another's ideological and philosophical outlook on things. For this type what is being presented just somehow makes sense to them. Often even unexplainably. That is okay, if it works for them. Some people are hardliners. Unmoved even in the face of strong evidence, sound reason, and irrefutable facts that contradict a previously held view. This type becomes so entrenched in their view that they consider themselves right even when they know they are wrong. But for them they are right and that is all that matters. And really, that is all that matters.

Sometimes we tend to try to force something down someone's throat. I'm not sure that's quite how it works. There is a natural and unnatural way of doing things. Naturally, when you eat something, there is a process by which this is done. You use a certain utensil, or your hands, depending on the type of food, either way only the amount that can be adequately chewed is put into the mouth. It is thoroughly chewed and then swallowed. It is a bit unnatural, not to mention unhealthy, to bite off more than you can chew and just wolf it down without masticating it properly. The same principle applies when 'advice' is forced down someone's throat. It is both unnatural and unhealthy.

Whether you find yourself on either end of this

spectrum of this right and wrong thing, or somewhere in between, you are the only one that can decide what is good for you. You know, sometimes the best advice you will ever get in life, is the advice you give yourself. Never overlook or underestimate that about yourself. The vantage point that you have of any situation is panameric, albeit subjective, it is a view that is more qualified to assess every part of the situation in ways that others are unable to. Whether you will be able to fully identify it or not, somehow when something is in your face, you will be able to recognize it as right or wrong for you.

(The Grand Finale)

Cards 40 – 52:

40. Appearances, 41. The Squeaky Wheel, 42. Birds of a Feather, 43. The Master of Trust and The Issue of Loyalty, 44. The Gift and The Curse, 45. Pyrrhic Victories, 46. New Realms of Possibilities, 47. Battle Concept, 48. Preventive Measures, 49. Contractual Obligations, 50. Effective Time Management, 51. Time, Place, Space Dynamic, 52. Modus Operandi

Card 40: Appearances

Appearance - External show: Semblance. Outward aspect.

*Concept/Objective: Appearances are generally deceptive. So you must train yourself to see beyond appearances and the many contradictions they contain. If not, you will be deceived at every turn. Seeing is far from believing.

(Questions)
1. What are some of the things that can be hidden in appearances?
2. Why are appearances so powerfully deceptive?
3. How can something appear one way, but in truth be something entirely different?

There are entire realities that can be hidden in appearances. Hidden in words. Hidden in gestures. Hidden in lifestyles. Unfortunately appearances can cover so much. We live in a world where anyone can be whoever they want to be and present that to the entire world as true. Why would we not believe what we see? If we had to always concern ourselves with having to determine whether or not someone was really who they portrayed themselves to be, we'd go crazy.

People are perception oriented and can be easily deceived into believing what they see. And this is why most people judge by appearances, you shouldn't. It is said that seeing is believing; well, if I can control what you see, then invariably I can control what you believe. Even if you know what you are looking at is not real, it makes no difference. This is how people are wired.

Magicians know this trick all too well. You can have an audience full of people watching intently every move the magician makes, and right in their face he pulls off an unbelievable act that, guess what?, is believed. It is hard not to believe what is before your eyes. How could it not be true? You're looking right at it? Don't be so easily duped. Always look beyond what is shown to you. Like the wizard of oz, look behind the curtain and you will see that things are not what they appear to be.

The power of appearances lies in the fact that you can create a reality that is not real. The power of appearances is that it allows you to be deceived or for you to deceive others. Knowing this, no one is beyond being deceived. Deception, on one level is not necessarily a bad thing. All warfare is based upon deception. You have to utilize whatever means that are at your disposal to conquer and overcome. This tradition is a long standing one. One that is time tested and proven to be effective.

There is no clearer arena to see this played out than that of war. 'If you are close to attacking, appear as though you are far away. If you are far away from attacking, appear as if you are close to attacking', and 'If you are weak, appear strong, and if your strong, appear weak.' 1. These tactical appearances are used to misdirect the enemy. This stance is temporal in nature, permanence has no place here. There must be a degree of fluidity in your movements. Once the purpose has been served and the season is over, cast those clothes aside in preparation for the next mission. Whatever you do, as with any climatic condition, dress appropriately and don the face for the occasion.

In appearances you have the ability to control the perceptions of others. What a powerful position to be in. Others may not know you, which is good, but they know what you appear to be. Unfortunately, this is exactly how people judge, by what seems to be rather than what actually is. Anyone can transform themselves to whatever or whoever they want to be. So it is hard to know who they really are. But there are indicators.

The best and most accurate of which is focusing on what someone does rather than what they say. People can drape themselves in as many different garbs as they want to. Actions and their effects will never steer you wrong. You measure the effects, nothing else. You measure what you don't see, by what you do see. This is purely mathematical. To get to the unknown, you simply work from that which is known. When something affects you, even if you can't readily see its origins, you know it

The Master's Deck

came from a real place.

Practiced dishonesty is more effective than unpracticed truth. You literally have people who have mastered the art of deception. They are master deceivers. They can take something that is one thing and give it the appearance of something else. Distraction is their key. By directing your focus elsewhere, they can do all sorts of things right in your face. Just like the magician. You will never see the sleight of hand or what is hidden up their sleeves.

An aspect of your real power lies in your ability to master the art of appearances. In order to infiltrate another's circle, you must learn the walk, the language, and the customs of that circle, so that it appears you are part and parcel. Be whatever the occasion calls for. Become flexible enough to come out of your world to enter theirs.

Why are people so deceptive? People perpetrate the fraud for many reasons. Mainly because they can? Perhaps they have a hidden agenda, or an ulterior motive? They could be hiding something about themselves they don't want you to know about? Or they are covering for some weakness they have? The reasons are endless.

Don't waste your time trying to figure it out because it really doesn't matter because you are not fooled by appearances anyway? You have learned to pierce the veil of the physical. You measure what's real, the effects, while not giving too much attention to surface things. If you look deep enough into anyone, no matter what you are looking for, you will find it. Everything exists in all of us in trace amounts. Some more in some than in others, but whatever it is, it is there, hidden deep within. Covered only by appearances.

* Key Points:
    a. There are entire realities that can be hidden in appearances
    b. Most people judge by appearances, but you shouldn't
    c. The power of appearances lies in the fact that you can create a reality that is not real
    d. No one is beyond being deceived
    e. You will always see what you are looking for in other people no matter what it is

Card 41: The Squeaky Wheel

Squeak - A shrill cry or noise. A distinct noise that is hard not to notice and give attention to.

* Concept/Objective: Closed mouths don't get fed. And the wheel that doesn't squeak doesn't get oiled. By remaining silent you make yourself invisible and unnoticeable. Make your presence known. In this case, silence is not golden, it will only make you forgotten. And anything forgotten gets ignored. Make some noise. Put yourself out there

(Questions)
1. What is the secret of asking for help?
2. Why does the squeaky wheel get oiled?
3. What can a baby teach you about squeaky wheels?

"A well-known principle of human behavior says that when we ask someone to do us a favor, we will be more successful if we provide a reason. People simply like to have reasons for what they do." 4

There is an art and science to everything. Asking for help is no different. The first thing to be determined is what kind of help you need? This is important because there are two primary concerns you need to address at the outset. First is who? Second is how? Who you ask for help matters. And how you ask for help matters. Let's deal with the first concern first. Who is willing and able to help you? Finding both of these factors in one person is key. Some are willing but are unable to provide you with the help you need. Others are able, but for one reason or another, are unwilling, or at least hesitant to help you. This is the dilemma you are up against.

What is your relationship to the one you need help from? Why should they help you? How do they benefit by helping you? Because they love you? Because they have a charitable spirit? Because in helping you they help themselves? Because they feel indebted to you? The list goes on. You must consider these things when searching for the right person to help you in your great time of need. It must be said that the type of help you need is one that is necessary to get you out of a dire situation or it could be to start a business venture. However, our primary focus here is on the former. But the principles under discussion applies to both.

The second concern we mentioned was how you ask for help. This may not seem so important, but not understanding this may cost you. There are both direct and indirect approaches. You see how this second concern ties into the first one mentioned above? Depending on the who, you can determine the how. The direct approach is reserved for those closest to you and it has been determined that they are both willing and able. The shortest distance between two points is a straight line. Just ask. There's no problem in the direct approach if it is applicable. It is the indirect approach that we need to give some attention to.

"...you are surrounded by people who absolutely have no reason to help you unless it is in their interest to do so." [3]

In all instances some would say that the best way to ask for help is simply to ask. Why beat around the bush? Sometimes it is not that simple. The question of why they should help you comes into play. Remember, they are able to help you, but are against helping you or somewhat reluctant to help you for a myriad of reasons, unless of course you uncover something in your request that they can benefit from. Self-Interest is the key that moves people and causes them to open their wallet up for you.

Finding out where the other persons interest lies will lower their resistance to you and your request. Most people are so preoccupied with their own lives and their own affairs that they can find no room for you in theirs. This is another reason why the direct approach will prove to be ineffective.

Did you know or do you believe that a request stated in one way will get rejected, while a request that asks for the same favor or help in a slightly different way is accepted? If that is the case, and it is, do you still think that how you ask for help doesn't really matter? Well it does. The sequential way in which you present your request must follow along a certain line. Give it some thought and develop a methodology that fits the person you need help from. Your ability to be tactful is crucial here. By this is meant that anything that works must be employed.

The squeaky wheel gets oiled because it squeaks. It is a sound that draws attention to itself. A sound that can't be ignored. Who can resist putting a little oil on a wheel that squeaks? No one. What is applicable here is not applicable under the concept of the Talking Skull. In that sense, there is danger in words. In this sense, there is safety, refuge, and salvation in words. When you are in danger or in need, there is no time to be silent. How will others know you need help if you don't ask? You have to ignore any and everything in you that serves as an impediment from you opening your mouth up. Focus on nothing but your objective.

Of all people, babies practice the squeaky wheel concept better than anyone. Babies instinctively understand that closed mouths don't get fed. Whether a baby needs to be fed, held, or changed; the who rarely matters, and they only know of one approach, direct. And until their need is met, you will hear a continuous cry. One that people can't help but come to the aid of. Learn from the baby. When all else fails be less discriminating of who you ask for help, and by all means, be direct.

* Key Points:

    a. There is a science and art to everything, including asking for help

    b. Who you ask for help matters and how you ask for help matters

    c. There are two approaches to asking for help, direct and indirect

    d. Since self-interest is the lever that moves people; uncover something in your request that the other can benefit from

    e. Focus on nothing but your objective

    f. Babies are good examples to follow when it comes to asking for help

Card 42: Birds of a Feather

Birds of a Feather - 'Birds of a Feather Flocking Together' is a natural congregation, gathering, or hanging around of people based upon strong ties, similarities, or other things they have in common.

* *Concept/Objective: You can tell a lot about a person by the company they keep. You will always be judged, fair or not, by those you surround yourself with. Association breeds similarities. Keep the wrong company or breed the wrong similarity and it could cost you.*

(Questions)
1. Why is it important to be mindful of the company you keep?
2. What makes it so easy for some people to gravitate to some people while not so much to others?
3. What is it about associations that they breed similarities?

The company you keep speaks volumes about who you are. You are known by the company you keep whether you like it or not. Even if they don't accurately reflect who you are, it makes no difference. It's called guilty by association. All this means is that you will be convicted by the court of public opinion for committing no offense at all other than choosing to deal with someone who may be in bad standings in the eyes of others. To convince others otherwise is pointless, futile, and a waste of your time. You might as well save your breath.

This association thing can work both ways. Just as you are judged by negative associations, you are also judged by positive ones as well. By surrounding yourself with positive, powerful, or productive people, it will give the impression that you are too even if it isn't the case at all. So, associations can work for you or against you. And this is why you should never just willynilly be in the company of others in a loose and carefree manner.

Birds of a feather really do flock together. And rare is the occasion when this is not the case. If it does happen it can be considered an anomaly, or at best, outside the realm of normalcy. That being said, ignore the cries of anyone who vehemently professes their disdain from being categorized in a certain light because of their deep social ties with someone or even their strong liking of someone.

In most cases there is some commonality or some admirable trait in that other person that allowed them to be attracted and or attached to them in the first place, if not then they would have been repulsed instead and shyed away from that other person or group rather than gravitated towards them. Most people prefer to be in the company of those they have the most in common with. This is true of any relationship.

The point here is that even if someone does not

have glaring traits or characteristics resembling someone they flock with, and by flock with I mean to be around someone for a considerable amount of time on a consistent basis, then this does not mean that these same traits and characteristics does not exist in them. They do exist. But they either hide them well, or they have them in lessor degrees, but you can rest assured they possess them no matter how bland their exteriors may be. It could even be an alter ego type of association where someone is, in their core, a certain way, but because of societal constraints, self image concerns, or their prudishness, they experience certain things vicariously through others who are less inhibited and or are less shameful.

There will be times when you may have to do business with someone who is known to have questionable character or is shady, you don't necessarily flock with them, but who you rub elbows with matters. Sadly, if you ever have to engage in any activity with someone whose character is unsavory, do it out of the gaze of others if your reputation could take a hit that you can't afford. Only do business with this type of person if there are no other alternatives available to you. Otherwise, unjust judgments may be cast upon you. However, depending upon the overall circumstances, to be determined by you, don't be swayed by how things look. Too much concern for outside opinions can impede you from a much needed blessing from an unlikely source.

Association breeding similarities is a natural phenomena that happens without any effort on your behalf at all. Your environment has a great impact on you in so many ways without your consent or knowledge. This impact is below the threshold of your awareness. These subtle influences becomes a part of you that you inherit from your surrounding conditions and those around you. Your mind cannot disengage itself completely from receiving and transmitting what surrounds it. Detachment can only be so effective. Remember the 'Irrevocable Power of Thought' and how your senses are the doorway by which enters the material that forms the basis of the thoughts you produce. There is no way this can be circumvented.

All in all, be careful of the people who you allow close to you, and be careful who you choose to be close to. It is not always true that just because someone has close social ties to someone that they are cut from the same cloth. There are limited exceptions to this rule, as there are with all rules. In these cases, they must be a beloved family member or a dear childhood friend. If either of these are true, you still should limit your ties with them if keeping their company will damage you reputation or can somehow prevent you from reaching a goal.

* Key Points:
   a. The company you keep speaks volumes about who you are. This will tell the world who you are whether you like it or not
   b. Birds of a feather really do flock together, let no one tell you otherwise
   c. Guilty by association can work for you or against you depending upon the type of company you keep
   d. Association breeds similarities is a natural phenomena that happens without any effort on your behalf
   e. Be careful of the people who you allow close to you, and be careful of who you choose to be close to

Card 43: The Matter of Trust and the Issue of Loyalty

Matter - Something under consideration.

Trust - To be able to rely on the character, ability, or truth of someone. To place confidence in.

Issue - A concern. A problem.

Loyalty - The state or condition of being loyal. Unswerving allegiance. Faithful.

* Concept/Objective: Be mindful that the vast majority of anyone you encounter, if not all, should be considered unworthy of your trust and loyalty. Consider wisely who you trust and be very concerned of those you think are loyal to you. Trust can happen, and

loyalty can exist, but neither of these should be looked forward to.

(Questions)
1. Why should matters of trust not be taken lightly?
2. What makes the issue of loyalty of supreme importance?
3. How or by what means can you determine how trustworthy or loyal someone is?

I once read something, and at the time of reading it, I found it difficult to fully understand. In fact, I disagreed with it. Not so much now. After much experience, deep reflection, and the passage of time, I had to take a second look at this previously held doubt. It said that, "Men will always be false unless compelled to be true."   7

Now imagine a world where not some, not most, but all men are false, fake, or untrue. For some this may be hard to wrap your mind around. However, it is for this reason, and this reason alone that matters of trust should not be taken lightly. Not at all. Your trust must never be given away freely at a mere whim. Earned trust is better. Even then, the rule is to never trust anyone completely. Because earned trust will get you burned too.

Your ability to easily trust or distrust depends on who you are, how you were raised, and the environment you grew up in. As can be seen in how John D. Rockefeller was dealt with by his father at an early age to instill in him an important principle. He used to jump from an elevated place into his father's arms. On one such occasion his father held his arms out to catch his son and pulled them away at the last second causing him to fall to the ground. His father told him sternly, "Remember, never trust anyone completely, not even me." 9

His father taught him a hard lesson which forged in him an approach towards future business endeavors that he never deviated from.

The relationship between trust and loyalty is inextricably linked. When you say that you trust someone, what are you really saying? You are saying you believe that the entrusted one can be relied upon to do what they say they are going to do or be who they say they are. That they will be faithful to you and will not betray you. In the right situation trust and loyalty can exist. But let your interests conflict with another's and you will see just how deep the seeds of betrayal can run.

The depth of deceit that some people will descend to will astonish you. Some people are callous beyond reason. With no thought other than to get what they want from whoever, whenever, however, and the world be dammed. Even if there is nothing to be gained, just seeing you fall is enough for some. It is difficult for many to comprehend this level of betrayal, but it exists. Often from the people you'd least expect. With this in mind, no one is beyond betraying you.

The greatest motivators of betrayal are many, they can range from jealousy, envy, and greed to strife and revenge, and even disappointment and dissatisfaction. These ingredients are the ultimate recipe for acts of betrayal. When you know someone possesses any of the above states of mind or tendencies, then seeking their trust and loyalty should be the furthest thing from your mind. Most people need a reason to act. The above factors are more than reason enough. Once someone betrays you it is hard to come back from. A host of cascading events can flow from one single act of betrayal. Consider the following:

In The Godfather, Don Corleone said that, "Treachery can't be forgiven. The one who has been betrayed can forgive, but people never forgive themselves and so they would always be dangerous. This type of forgiveness by the one betrayed would be like shirking his duty to himself and his family. They would have been a danger to everyone...all our lives." 8

Once you betray someone, you know that you have brought upon yourself a well-deserved consequence by the one you betrayed. So you can't imagine being forgiven. You think it is a trick and meant to deceive you into letting your guard down that will open you up to an attack. I will leave it to the reader to determine for him or herself how to deal with treachery. Just be very aware.

The specific standard you use to determine the trustworthiness or loyalty of someone is entirely up to you. But whatever standard you use, it must never be compromised. Tests reveal results. This barometer of weighing, measuring, tagging, and labeling is the surest way to ascertain who is who and what is what.

Small circles are the best and only way to avoid widespread betrayal. Yet, distance produces potential for betrayal too. This may seem contradictory, but both statements are true. The closer someone is to you relationship wise, then that personal connection makes it more difficult to ignore the ties that bind. The more remote someone is from you then this lack of personal attachment facilitates all sorts of happenings. At the same time, it makes those in your inner circle the most dangerous because it is only those closest to you that can harm you the most. Still, the smaller the circle the better.

More often than not we have a tendency to trust those we know the most. Unfortunately, disloyalty is more common than you think. The easiest way for someone to deceive you is to gain your trust. The cloak of familiarity is a guise most difficult to protect yourself from. All this means is that the closer people get to you the more you need to test them. Misplaced trust will be the leading cause of your downfall. Never be in a rush to trust.

Human beings are infallible and subject to anything. Don't put anything past anyone. In the end all you have is yourself. Don't get me wrong, you do have some genuinely good people. Others, if it is good for them to be so, only act good. Rare is the man who is virtuous. He flaunts it not. You have to have an eye for him when he crosses your path. Finding this type of person is far and in between. It is like finding a needle in a haystack. Integrity is an innate trait. Either you have it or you don't.

Arming yourself with true friends is the strongest defense against conspiratorial attacks and acts of betrayal. When it is all said and done, a person's allegiance is to himself. To expect anything other than that is both foolish and naive. The key thing is to limit those situations where you can be betrayed by putting into practice certain preventive measures as outlined in card forty-eight.

Success in any form, or to any degree, sets the stage for betrayal. It sets the stage for anyone to move against you. Their plotting can take many forms and can be on any level. So when you have, no matter what it is; whether it's money, power, material possessions, respect, a talent, and another does not have, be alert and aware to your surroundings and the people who occupy it because if any of these factors exists for you, then another's mind is potentially ripe for betrayal. So, pay attention to subtleties. Those signs that indicate to you that someone will cross you, double cross you, or even triple cross you.

Key Points:
   a. Trust no one completely
   b. No one is beyond betraying you
   c. Disloyalty is more common than you think
   d. Misplaced trust is one of the leading causes of a person's downfall
   e. A person's allegiance is ultimately to himself
   f. Arming yourself with true friends is the best defense against conspiratorial attacks
   g. Success in any form, or to any degree sets the stage for betrayal

Card 44: The Gift and the Curse

Gift – A notable capacity, talent, or endowment. To endow with some power, quality, or attribute. To be the recipient of something good. A blessing.

Curse – An evil or misfortune. A cause of great harm or misfortune. To bring great evil upon.

* Concept/Objective: An exceptional talent, quality, or ability can bring you great joy and success. That same talent, quality, or ability can also be the means of your demise or destruction. Sometimes, you just have to take the bitter with the sweet. Or do you? Not necessarily in all cases. There is a way to keep your gift a gift.

(Questions)

1. How can something be both a gift and a curse?

2. What does the phrase, "a blessing in disguise," really mean?
3. Why must you be cruel only to be kind?

Sometimes a gift, skill, or talent that you are born with, or one you acquire or develop at some point in your life, can also become the cause of misfortune as well. However, this does not have to be the case. Because knowing how something can be used against you, even something you have been blessed with, allows you the means to protect yourself from anything or anyone that can be exploitive of that blessing.

There are many gifts to make our point, but let us look at the following: You have goodness, beauty, loyalty, fame, power, and free will to name a few. Without even having to delve deep off into any of these, peripherally alone, general conclusions can be drawn from your own life to see how any of these can work for you and against you. Let's take under analysis only one of these—the gift of goodness—to see how although goodness is by all measures a good trait or attribute to have, it still can, under certain circumstances, work against you.

At first glance, to mention that being good can be both a gift and a curse may be surprising to some. If you fit in this group, then you just may be living in a bubble. Or your life has been so sheltered that you are oblivious to some of the harsh realities of life and some of the mean-spirited people who live in it. There are many ravenous people who are wolves in sheep's clothing seeking to take advantage of anyone they are able.

Just try being too good around the wrong person, and you will soon see how your own goodness can work against you. A genuinely good person who only sees good in other people is a conman's best friend. You have people who have made it their profession to prey on the goodness of others. This is why you have fake charities and all sorts of scams out there that gullible people fall for without fail.

Some people are good because they just are. Some are good because they feel they have to be because of their upbringing and to be other than good would go against what has been instilled in them all their life. They have not been scarred by a whole lot of bad experiences that makes them look at the world any differently. Sadly, you have to guard your own goodness in a world like this. It's unfortunate but true. Being surrounded by so many animalistic types of people, you have to transform yourself so that your own humanity does not work against you.

"...since anyone who would act up to a perfect standard of goodness in everything, must be ruined among so many who are not good. It is essential, therefore, for a Prince who desires to maintain his position, to have learned how to be other than good, and to use or not to use his goodness as necessity requires..." (7)

Historically, the greatest triumphs, the most creative works, and the biggest societal impacts have been born out of a tragedy, some type of hardship, or just an overall bad experience. So it should be no wonder how something good can come from something not so good. There is always, if you have an eye for it, a silver lining in almost everything that is considered bad. It's all a matter of perspective. How you look at something will determine if you are either weighed down by it or able to benefit from it.

In addition, how you go through or experience a trying ordeal or troubling time affects your ability to mine that experience for its hidden treasures, which are always there despite the severity of the experience. But the pain of the moment causes our focus to be on the pain rather than the good that is inherent in it. I know that it is hard to imagine that even in tragedy there is hope, but there is. The hope or the good is disguised, so it is not easily seen. It wouldn't be called a blessing "in disguise" if you could see it just by looking at it. This is why you have to look beyond, behind, and underneath a thing to see the blessing in it for you.

The dichotomy here is that, just as good can be a gift and a curse, bad can also be a cause of some harm or the pathway to a blessing. The key thing to keep in mind is that in either case, you are the determining factor as to how any of these situations works out for you.

Cruelty is not cruel if the purpose behind your cruelty is kindness. This is not a play on words, although this basic premise does come from a play. Some take advantage of kind-spirited and generous people. They feel you owe them because of your relationship to them. And the more you give, the more they take; and the more they take, the more they expect to receive. There should be limits that you set to how far you extend yourself to others.

"You should never stop exercising your compassion Have love in your heart, but be smart and express your compassion with restraint...out of your desire to be kind, you expose yourself without a protective shield. Strange but true, we often abuse those who support and love us the most." (5)

You must take a firm stand at times that may rub a few people the wrong way, but better to do that than be overly nice for the sake of not wanting to offend or seem to be rude and be misused in the process. It is preferable to be uneasy through perceived cruelty now than to suffer greater later as a result of being too accommodating.

So, your harsh position is more of a defensive posture and one where you are operating from a position of strength, not weakness. It's a protective measure. You don't want to allow yourself to be misused by anyone taking advantage of your kind and giving nature. Don't be anyone's doormat. And sometimes for you not to be that, you have to be cruel, or at least the appearance of it.

Imagine a parent being too compassionate, loving, and caring towards their child to the point that they don't discipline that child even though they know they should. They don't want their child to hurt or suffer. They don't want to hurt the child's feelings. But it is much wiser to punish the child and cause a little pain now to protect the child from a much more severe punishment in the future from society, which you will neither have the power or control to help them from or out of. Be cruel in order to be kind.

One more cautionary note and excuse that may look like an absurd proposition, but be aware of so-called "kind and honest" men. Feigned kindness and honesty are two of the hardest ruses to protect you from. These types of people can be some of the most deceitful and dangerous people around. Hidden behind their nice smile and bland exterior is potential evil. This does not mean that you look for evil, but you are ever-alert to any potential harm, no matter what form it expresses itself in or through.

Kindness and honesty can disarm more effectively than almost anything else, so all the more reason to be alert. They are nonthreatening gestures, therefore they raise no immediate red flags. To you, however, especially at this stage of your readings, non-glaring signs are just as signaling as the more open ones. Much of this was discussed previously in card forty.

* **Key Points:**
    a. Gifts, skills, and talents can work for you or against you.
    b. Be good, but not gullible.
    c. There is always, if you have an eye for it, a silver lining in almost everything that is considered bad.
    d. How you go through or experience an ordeal or trying time affects your ability to mine that experience for the hidden treasures it contains.
    e. Cruelty is not cruel if the purpose behind your crudely is kindness.
    f. Feigned kindness and honesty are the greatest ruses to protect yourself from.

Card 45: Pyrrhic Victories

Pyrrhic – Achieved at excessive cost. Costly to the point of negating or outweighing expected benefits.

Victory – The overcoming of an enemy. Achievement of mastery or success in a struggle or endeavor against odds or difficulties.

Pyrrhic Victory – In 279 B.C., Pyrrhus, the king of Epirus, defeated the Romans at the battle of

Ausculum, but lost all his top officers and many men. He said after the battle, "one more such victory and we are lost." (15)

Concept/Objective: Determine when you should move as it relates to factoring in benefits and losses. This is more crucial than many realize. Think. Reflect. Strategize. Weigh. After all of that, decide and then act, but only if your win is a win and does not end up hurting you.

(Questions)
1. How can a win really be a loss?
2. In what way can you guard against Pyrrhic victories?
3. Under what circumstances does it not matter how much loss you sustain?

On the surface, it may seem paradoxical to win and lose at the same time, but Pyrrhic victories are more common than most think, and they are more costly than any temporal win or gain. The devastating effects can, at times, be far greater than all your small wins combined. Every win is not a win; some are well-clothed losses. All in all, there are four dynamics to this, and they are: a win-win situation; a lose-lose situation; a win-lose situation; and a lose-win situation. What you want is the win-win or the lose-win situation because in the end, you want to win. This brings us back to winning at all costs, which means not losing at any cost.

There are many examples that can be given to illustrate how a win can be a loss. While I'm sure the reader is well aware of what a Pyrrhic victory is, I still think it is best to give an example. One that I think many people can relate to is during arguments. Many of us have been there. Yes, arguments. Getting the best of an argument at the expense of losing respect or friendship because of offending someone in the process is very common. Offending someone can be potentially dangerous on many levels, but all that mattered to you was being right. It made you feel good. The damage done to some relationships is irreparable. You won the argument, but loss so much more. This is your typical win-lose situation.

Then you have those lose-lose situations, when no matter what you decide to do, there is no positive outcome. You are damned if you do; damned if you don't. The only action here is what you do to prevent from being in these types of situations in the first place if you can help it.

What would you rather do, win every battle and lose the war; or lose every battle and win the war? The answer may be obvious, but many times, we become so fixated on one particular matter at hand that we are determined not to lose at that one thing, not knowing or even considering distant or long-term negative implications. It can be difficult to factor in intangibles, but you must. Those who are able to do this are of an elite class. The crux of this revolves around the ever-so-important principle of measuring everything by what it costs you. How?

Weighing the pros and cons of any situation is a good start. This will help you make better decisions before going beyond the point of no return, and this will also guide you in a less costly course of action. In the above example dealing with arguments, even if it is not readily obvious, small hints and signs shown to you at any stage prior to or during your exchange with the other person should have been enough of an indicator for you stop before things get worse.

The primary way to guard against Pyrrhic victories is to always consider consequences. Weigh things out, in advance. Ask yourself, "If I do succeed, at what cost? What can I lose even if I win?" And if you can afford to pay the price, then by all means, go ahead; indulge yourself. But if the fox is not worth the chase, then this tells you that you need to think better of taking a certain action that can hurt you more than help you. Don't let the prospect of gain blind you to act against your own best interest. This is why having control of your emotions is very important. Greed is a great enticer. Our appetite for something, or even someone, can cause us to throw caution to the wind and dive headfirst into a no-win situation. By the time we realize it, it's too late.

As a last resort, especially when you are all out of options, go all in. This is really the only time it is even remotely wise to cast aside the cost factor. In fact, not to act would be more costly than if you did. You will know when it is time not to be cautious or measured in your actions because your back will be against the wall and there will be only one direction to go. Forward. At this point, consequences are irrelevant. This is the reverse aspect to this card. You can only benefit when you are forced to act, even if you do take a loss. A loss is not the same as losing. You can take a loss and still be winning.

Other than the scenario just mentioned, you have the opportunity to always experience a win-win situation. Why else would time be taken out to introduce a card of this theme if it was not within your reach to do so? Everything has to be in perfect alignment for a win-win situation. Don't be dismayed by a loss; some losses are cleverly clothed wins, just as some wins are cleverly hidden losses. Losses lead to wins, depending on any number of factors—mainly you. Sometimes you have to go backwards before you can go forward. Even if you do have to take a loss, so be it. You tried.

* **Key Points:**
    a. Always measure everything by what it costs you.

b. Be careful: Every win is not a win; sometimes, it is a well-clothed loss.
c. Consider consequences before taking action.
d. Winning some arguments is a good example of a Pyrrhic victory.
e. Don't let the prospect of gain blind you against your own best interest.
f. When you have no other recourse, consequences don't matter; go all in.

Card 46: New Realms of Possibility, The Sky's the Limit

New – Having recently come into existence. Recent; modern.

Realm – Sphere; domain.

Possible – Being within the limits of ability, capacity, or realization. Capable of happening or occurring.

Sky – The upper atmosphere or expanse of space that constitutes an apparent great vault or arch over the Earth. Upper regions.

Limit – Something that bounds, restrains, or confines.

*Concept/Objective: There is nothing that is not accomplishable. Anything is possible in this dispensation of time. The only thing holding you back is yourself. The self-imposed limitations we foist upon ourselves are more restrictive than anything anyone else can do to us. You have a responsibility to do what

your heart desires. Anything else is an affront to your God-given talents and abilities.

(Questions)
1. What is it that makes things impossible?
2. How can you enter into new realms of possibility?
3. Why are self-imposed limitations the worst of all?

"With men things are impossible, but with God nothing is impossible." (10)

Impossibility lies in the fact that you are without the knowledge of God by whatever name you call Him: God, Allah, Jehovah, the Creator... It makes no difference. If you know who God is, in essence and in truth, then it will develop in you a mindset that knows no limitations whatsoever. Why? Because what you'll discover is His essence at the very core of your being. Can you imagine God incapable of doing anything? No. Nothing is impossible for God. When you connect and become one with that essence, what spirit do you think you'll embody? What new realms do you think you will grow into? The realm where everything now becomes possible because the spirit that drives you is of and from the Originator of it all.

This does not mean that you will not have to

put the necessary work in or that you won't experience difficulties and setbacks, but it does open a door for you that you never knew existed. With this newfound knowledge, you come into the realization that you can accomplish whatever you put your mind to. It sounds easy, doesn't it? But it really is that simple. Being deprived of this kind of knowledge will always hold you back and keep you dependent on the knowing ones.

Once this knowledge begins to enter into you, your mind will expand to unimaginable proportions, and you will enter into a domain where you exercise your dominance unrestricted. Never underestimate the power of something new. This new sphere of activity, which is from above, will be so superior that all you can do is accomplish things of great magnitude. This is where you can honestly say that there really is nothing between you and your goals except air and opportunity. How much resistance will air be to you other than the natural force of gravity?

The force of gravity needs to be fought against. It is a force that is unseen, but not unreal. Gravity has the force and the power to hold you back and keep you down. But it is one that must be overcome if you are to ascend to new heights. There are also forces within you that are unseen, but not unreal, just as those outside of you. These forces also have the potential to greatly interfere with your vertical rise, therefore they, too, must be successfully contended with if you are to rise into the upper regions of your mind.

When you begin to move on a level not experienced by most, so many opportunities will be opened up for you. Not to mention those you make for yourself. Opportunities will be everywhere. You will be surrounded by them. Even in trying situations, opportunities are present. No matter how tragic an ordeal may be that you are going through, there is always a silver lining. I know that they can be difficult to see, but they definitely are there.

What happens when one door closes? Right. Another one opens. We have experienced this in one way or another. Imagine if that door had not been closed, we would have never discovered what was behind the door that was opened to us. This makes unexpected opportunities sometimes the best ones because they yield the greatest results and contain the greatest blessings. Protect yourself from missed opportunities.

How are opportunities lost?

"Generally speaking, opportunities are lost through misinformation or lack of information, faulty evaluation of intelligence, lack of courage or initiative, indolence, preoccupation, or similar flaws in basic management...there are three avenues of opportunity: events, trends, and conditions: When opportunities occur through events but you are unable to respond, you are not smart. When opportunities become active through a trend and yet you cannot make plans, you are not wise. When opportunities emerge through conditions but you cannot act on them, you are not bold." (1)

And lastly, you are already confronted on every side with those who cast upon your restraints; restraints that limit you. Why would you compound that by imposing limitations on yourself? There is no greater enemy to you achieving your goals other than you. When you get out of the way of your own progress by successfully dealing with those forces we spoke of earlier, then the skies really will be the limit for you—which is no limit at all. Nothing will be impossible for you when you enter these new realms of possibility.

* Key Points:
- a. Impossibility lies in the fact that you are without the knowledge of God.
- b. With the knowledge of God, you will come into the realization that you can accomplish whatever you put your mind to.
- c. Your mind will be expanded to unimaginable proportions where you enter a domain where you will exercise your dominance unrestricted.
- d. The force of gravity, both internally and externally, needs to be successfully contended

with if you are to rise.

e. Many opportunities will cross your path, so be ready to capitalize off them, or they could be lost.

f. Of all the limitations that exist, those that are self-imposed are the worst of all.

Card 47: Battle Concept

Battle – A combat between two persons. An extended contest, struggle, or controversy.

Concept – Something conceived in the mind; thought, notion, or idea. Organized around a main idea or theme.

*Concept/Objective: Your mind is one of the greatest weapons you have, and often the most underutilized. Properly affixing your mind to combat what life will throw at you is crucial. There will always be struggles that you will face; better to embody a concept that will allow you to win. A battle concept.

(Questions)

1. What is a battle concept?
2. Why is it dangerous to be ignorant of military affairs?
3. Why is martial training a necessary component of the battle concept?

By battle concept, what I want to highlight is the idea of war and the idea of militancy. It embodies a mindset where you approach every situation like a soldier. It is being preoccupied with warlike pursuits. Contrary to what may be perceived and keeping with the theme of this book, each card's primary focus is dealing with the mind more than anything else. Your struggle and combativeness is with yourself. This will make any external battle of non-effect. This reminder should assist you as you read this card. The goal is for you to never be unprepared for anything at any time and to combat anything effectively should it arise. We will cover this more as we proceed. First, I want to give you a glimpse into the state of military affairs and its pursuits, from a historical perspective.

"...a Prince, therefore, should have no care or thought but for war, and for the regulations and training it requires, and should apply himself exclusively to this, for war is the sole art looked for in one who rules. So to be proficient in it is the surest way to acquire power. A Prince, who is ignorant of military affairs, besides other disadvantages, can neither be respected by his soldiers, nor can he trust them. A Prince, therefore, ought never to allow his attention to be diverted from warlike pursuits and should occupy himself with them even more in peace than in war. This can be done in two ways, by practice or by study." (7)

Studying war is good, but study alone won't suffice. It is only when you practice the ways of war that it produces an instantaneous understanding of your war studies, as is the case with all studies. Study and its application have always been intertwined. Each one makes the other more significant. In time, your superiority will be unmatched. The superior militarist is one who is able to "win before he even has to fight." This is the ultimate objective of one who has embraced and embodied the battle concept philosophy. You have to think your way through situations.

The above can only happen if you train yourself in the ways of war. This is what makes martial training a necessary component. Martial training deals with anything pertaining to war and its characteristics. I would like to introduce the following acronym for the word "martial" to highlight these characteristics: Militant, Armed, Readiness, Tactics, Industrious, Alert, Loyal. As someone who trains and conditions themselves for war, you should always be militant, armed, ready, tactful, industrious, alert, and loyal.

Being militant is having a mental disposition that combats any hostile force that seeks to do you harm. This is more internal than anything else. Every soldier needs weaponry, so arm yourself with the right knowledge that will allow you to vanquish any opposition against you. Anything can happen at any time, from anyone, at any place; this is why being constantly in a state of readiness is important.

Tactics is having the ability to apply whatever

measures are necessary that will effectively deal with any matter without relying on any one set method to accomplish this. This means being fluid and flexible enough to adopt an approach befitting the occasion. Anything that works is considered a good tactic.

Being industrious is staying busy engaging in worthy pursuits because time is precious, and it takes constant work to achieve your goals. What you are really doing is battling laziness. Alertness is practiced to such a degree that it keeps your senses heightened and aware to any impending threat or danger, wherever it may be or whoever it may come from. Never being unalert means never getting caught off guard.

Lastly there is loyalty. To whom? To what? Be loyal to yourself. A lot of people are guilty of betraying themselves. This is more common than you think. This betrayal comes in the form of giving up on yourself and settling for less, thereby selling yourself short instead of fighting through struggles to finish what you set out to do. Be loyal to whatever you have committed yourself to. Don't sway. Be dedicated and unswerving. These are universal characteristics of war that embody the concept of battle that is applicable to everyone. If for some reason you think that these characteristics don't apply to you, then think again.

It might surprise you to know that you are a

soldier by nature. You were born to fight and struggle. You had to fight and struggle to be born. Had you not gone to war with various forces inside the womb of your mother, you would have never completed the journey to be here. Now that you are here, why stop fighting and struggling against similar forces that are keeping you from emerging into a greater expression of yourself? Even though there are external forces to contend with, the forces that reside right within you are the ones that need to be fought against the most. First within, then without. You will not be as victorious over that which is without unless you are victorious over that which is within.

* Key Points:
    a. The idea of war and militancy is at the root of what a battle concept is.
    b. Your struggle and combativeness are with yourself.
    c. Always be militant, armed, ready, tactful, industrious, alert, and loyal.
    d. You are a soldier by nature.
    e. First within, then without.

Card 48: Preventive Measures

Prevent – To meet or satisfy in advance. To act ahead. To keep from happening or existing.

Measure – To choose or control with cautious restraint. To regulate by a standard.

*Concept/Objective: How do you know what is going to happen until it happens? You don't. But you can take measures in advance against anything that is likely or probable of happening. Your ability to foresee and anticipate possibilities will aid you in such measures. Failure to act in advance can be costly in the long run.

(Questions)

1. When planning for preventive measures, how should you prioritize your planning?
2. What is the general purpose of a preventive measure? What determines the effectiveness of such a measure?
3. What can be done if a preventive measure was not taken or does not work? In other words, what other steps can be taken?

Primarily, what you want to focus on here is setting general measures that are intended to greatly reduce, minimize, or eradicate completely potential problems. When something is general, it involves, is applicable to, or affects the whole of something or someone. It means basic or rudimentary. There are basic things you can do to prevent the existence of problems that can affect you prior to them even arising. There are too many uncontrollable aspects of life that are beyond your reach or control. The one thing you can have a degree of control over is yourself. No one else.

Therefore, your planning should begin and end with you. Priority number one is you: how you move; how you present yourself to others; how you interact with others; who you choose to affiliate yourself with; who you commit to; what you commit to. These are all important factors in prevention. The devil is definitely in the details. You can't afford to ignore anything. The smallest thing can make the biggest difference, especially when it comes to the points of contact mentioned above.

You can do everything right, but if your preventive measures did not serve to avoid or keep certain things from happening, then they were ineffective. You can tell the effectiveness of anything by what it produces. Potentially contentious situations are always afoot, so having a good understanding of why conflicts exists in the first place will help you in formulating the proper approach or appropriate way in how you do what you do.

Most conflicts exist because of the lack of something like: a lack of respect; a lack of understanding; a lack of a need being met; and so on. For example, in friendships, if someone feels they have been disrespected; in business, if either party misunderstands certain terms; or in relationships, if either partner fails to give the other what the other needs. In understanding this, you give everyone their proper respect, you always make sure that there are no misunderstandings, and you are mindful of what your partner's needs are.

There are primarily five stages involved when handling conflicts, with small variances.

They are:

1. Preventive measures;
2. Conflict resolution;
3. Minimizing collateral damage;
4. Damage assessment; and
5. Damage control.

Preventive measures are the best remedy for potential conflicts. However, if a preventive measure was not taken in advance of something or if the preventive measure you did take failed to be effective, then there are other steps that can be taken to limit the potential damaging effect of a situation or conflict. Obviously your first line of defense is to prevent.

Secondly, if that measure fails or proves to be inadequate, you make every effort to resolve the conflict before it advances even further. This is where conflict resolution is practiced. When a situation has gotten to this point, it is critical that a resolution is reached because if not, then the inevitable will occur, which is a continued strain between those involved, or at worst, confrontation.

Active participation of all parties involved is absolutely essential during this stage if there is to be any resolution at all. Now, something caused the conflict, so step one is to clearly identify what the problem is; have it clearly explained. It is possible to have a situation where you or the person has no idea they offended or wronged the other person or whatever the issue is. If it is just that simple, then a quick recognition and clarification can perhaps suffice. Beyond that, more technical steps need to follow.

Once the problem is identified, next there needs to be acceptance of the problem because if one side says, "Yes, that is the problem," and the other side says, "No, that is not the problem," then the process to resolve the problem is brought to a halt. Ultimately, whichever party was wrong in the situation must be willing to do whatever it takes to fix the problem. One of the hardest things for anyone to do is to admit that they were or are wrong. It takes a courageous person to admit fault. Along with strength, honesty is also required. Sometimes the shame involved makes it uneasy to honestly face a problem head on.

There is also an emotional component involved: anger. Things have a tendency of getting heated when conflict is present. The people directly involved in the problem or conflict should not be left alone to solve the problem by themselves because of this. This is why, in an ideal situation, it would include the presence of a qualified, concerned, and unbiased mediator who can mediate the situation. This person listens without judging, helps to clarify points, and brings order to the discussion.

Since you don't want to be unprepared if your conflict resolution sessions fails to work, you have to foresee the unfolding of events and go to the next step of dealing with a problematic issue that is on its way to spiraling out of control. This next step is minimizing collateral damage—before the fact, not after. The idea is to limit the range and effect of a loss because of a dispute or confrontation.

Naturally, the dispute at hand, be it legal, business, or on a more personal level like with friends or family, must come to a head at this stage of the conflict. There is no getting around the issue. The thing to remember is to only use whatever resources are needed. Anything beyond what is necessary can result in causing excessive harm, loss, or damage that could have been avoided by using only what was needed to remedy the problem. Once this has taken place, it's on to the next step.

Now is when you take a hard look at what has just transpired. How much damage was done will let you know how and what needs to be repaired. Basically, a full and adequate assessment is required so that your restructuring, restoring, and reorganizing efforts are properly directed and focused on much needed areas.

Lastly, damage control: This is a measure to offset or lessen the damage to reputation, credibility, or public image caused by a controversial act, remark, or revelation. A little ingenuity is required here. Tactfully do what is needed to counter and/or fix the effects of the conflict based upon your assessments done at stage four.

There is no "be all to end all" solutions when handling conflicts. However, a large percentage of problems that you encounter in life are largely avoidable by prevention. Become effective at each stage of handling conflicts; there will be enough things in your life that are unforeseen and unplanned for that will keep you busy or away from other matters of importance. You shouldn't compound things by not doing all within your power and ability to effectively prevent the things you can.

* **Key Points:**
    a. You are priority one in establishing preventive measures.
    b. Potentially contentious situations are always afoot.
    c. Preventive measures are the best remedy for potential conflict.
    d. Clearly identify problems that need to be resolved.
    e. Become functional at each stage of handling conflict.

Card 49: Contractual Obligations

Contract – A binding agreement between two or more people.

Obligation – The action of obligating oneself to a course of action or cause (as by a promise or vow). A commitment.

*Concept/Objective: Not giving your word is better than giving it and not keeping it. There is no getting around your word. In one way or another, you will be held accountable. Your loss will be immeasurable and unimaginable when you fail to remain committed to contractual terms.

(Questions)
1. Under what circumstances are you not bound by a contractual obligation?
2. Why must you always make your word bond (except in regard to the above question no. 1)?
3. What is an unsolicited contractual obligation, and in what ways do they bind you against your will?

The circumstances that substantiate you from not being charged with a breach of contract is when the thing that made you give your word in the first place no longer exists. In other words, when the other party or parties have been unfaithful or dishonest in any sense, then you not only have the right, but a duty to yourself to deal with them accordingly. To subject yourself to previously agree upon terms while others have not is unwise and can cause you harm in the long run. Your obligation then becomes the opposite of your initial agreement. This is what makes an annulment necessary. When you don't divorce yourself from unworthy entanglements, then you will always get the short end of the stick.

Did you know that when someone gives their word, that is a contractual obligation? I know that when someone thinks about contracts, they think about a piece of paper that discusses terms to be agreed upon. The vast majority of contracts surprisingly are unwritten, and they involve a handshake or the giving of your word. Your word is a part of who you are. Your ability to keep your word reveals what type of character you have. Many people, for one reason or another, give their word, and many people, for one reason or another, break their word. Anyone who breaks their word is untrustworthy.

A contract is a binding agreement: Your word binds you; and not keeping with your contractual obligations is considered a breach of contract, a breach of trust, and you are charged with acting in bad faith. When you breach your contract, there are penalties that are enforceable by the rule of law—written and unwritten. This enforcement can take many forms. Just know that you will always be held accountable for your nonfeasance.

Now, are there times when you are prevented from keeping your word, where factors outside of your control exist that interfere in such a way that you can't fulfill your obligations? Yes. These are contingents that excuse you. But once those contingents are removed, then you must do whatever it takes to fulfill your obligations. No one wants to deal with someone who can't keep their word. Can you blame them? This is why it is often better not to give your word than to give it and not live up to it. You'd be surprised how much can be lost when you mess up your standing with people when you do this. A man who does not keep his word is a liar, and a liar can't be trusted. The last thing you want is a reputation for is being a liar. Even then, strangely enough, this is preferable to some for any number of reasons.

Human psychology dictates that we feel a sense of duty—an obligation, if you will—to return to another who has bestowed upon us a gift or favor. This is called the rule of reciprocity. We tend to reciprocate to others a gift, a kind act, or a favor. It is a form of indebtedness.

"Another person can trigger a feeling of indebtedness by doing us an uninvited favor." (4)

So, if you know that something is being offered to you without you requesting it, and know that accepting the offer will bind you in some way to that individual, then why would you accept it in the first place? This again is part of the three-prong aspect of the rule of reciprocity.

"There is an obligation to give, an obligation to receive, and an obligation to repay." (4)

All contracts have two parts: offer and acceptance. When someone offers you anything and you accept it, in that act, you bind yourself in some way to the one who presented the offer. You have to fight against the natural inclination to accept or receive. If you don't want to be exploited, then steer clear of these types of unsolicited contractual obligations. The further you travel down the road with someone who subtly foists upon you favors, the more difficult they become to reject. A person is more capable of rejecting during the beginning stages of a relationship as opposed to if they wait further along in the relationship, and it is easier to reject something from a total stranger than it is from someone who you know or have some ties with.

Never underestimate the hidden power in favors. In the same way that the rule of reciprocity can work against you, it can also work for you. Any good businessman looks for a healthy return on his investments. A small favor can turn into something much greater than what was bestowed. You have to find the right situation and the right person in order for this to work. Everyone is wired different psychologically. In saying that, some don't stick to so-called psychological norms, and when it comes time for them to reciprocate, they don't feel any inclination whatsoever to return a favor. They will take and take and take. This is the exception, not the rule.

Lastly, don't allow others to force you into committing to them. Just as much as you should reject unsolicited favors, you should also reject unsolicited requests. Never feel compelled to do for others except it be by your own choosing. Remember, the fewer the commitments the better.

* **Key Points:**
   a. Don't obligate yourself to those who are unworthy.
   b. Make your word your bond.
   c. Contracts are enforceable by law.
   d. Be wary of unsolicited favors and unsolicited requests.

Card 50: Effective Time Management

Effective – Producing a decided, decisive, or desired effect.

Time – The measured or measurable period during which an action, process, or condition exists or continues.

Manage – To handle or direct with a degree of skill.

*Concept/Objective: Of all things recoverable, time is not one of them. Discipline of mind and clarity of focus is greatly needed. Waste not, want not. Idleness is the playground for underdeveloped minds to frolic

around in. You have no such luxury. Get busy and stay busy. You have no time to waste.

(Questions)
1. What are some of the things you must contend with when it comes to managing your time effectively?
2. How valuable are managerial skills when it comes to the concept of time?
3. What type of mindset must you have to make the best use of your time?

"There are very few men...and they are the exceptions...who are able to think and feel beyond the present moment." (2)

Time is measured in moments. Too many times, we get so caught up in the moment that it blinds us to our future plans being foiled or derailed. By thinking beyond the present moment, you won't allow any momentary situation, no matter how pleasurable or painful it is, to cause you to be distracted. Always having something to work towards can help you stay on course despite whatever may come your way. Never invest too much in the present without regard for the future.

There are actually 23 hours, 56 minutes, and 46 seconds in a day. There is only so much time to go around. The main problem you will run into is dispersing and spreading your time out between many things and many people. This ill can be cured by prioritizing, not taking on too many tasks at once, and not having too many unnecessary commitments.

Procrastination is another form of waste to be guarded against when it comes to time. When you know there is something you should be doing, do it. Putting things off when they're able to be done right now will only put you behind the eight ball later on.

Unnecessary and involuntary idleness, which is deeply embedded in the human psyche in the form of non-consequential leisure time activities, should be avoided. On a whole, there is nothing wrong with a little relaxation, entertainment, or outings that temporarily take you away from the mundaneness of your life. Demanding too much of yourself is not the wisest thing. Just be practical in how you distribute your most valuable resource: time. Take whatever time is necessary to recharge, rejuvenate, and recuperate. This is crucial for sustained productivity. Otherwise, you will suffer from burnout, and fatigue will set in that can put you in a prolonged slump that is hard to get out of.

The point here is being able to find the right balance. This is why managerial skills are needed when it comes to the concept of time and how you spend yours. The key word is "spend." Unlike money, when you spend your time, you are giving something up that is not recoverable. This makes it very necessary to spend your time on things or people that will bring you the greatest joy and return.

Good planning is important in managing your time effectively. You should always know what you are going to be doing from moment to moment. Moments add up, and before you know it, you have wasted a lot of time figuring out what is next on your agenda. A good practice is to plan in advance. Know beforehand what you will be doing the next day, the next week, or the next month, etc.

This not only saves you time; it keeps your energies focused. By the time you rise up in the morning, you should already know what you are going to be doing for that day. At the end of the day, plan for the next. You would be surprised at how effective just this one thing can be. The only problem you will run into is a distraction here and there and other unexpected happenings or even emergencies. Take them as they come.

Time is precious. There is no time to be lazy. Don't rush, yet always move with a sense of urgency. With that said, stay at it and allow no time for nonsense while you are in the midst of any major project. Give it the time and attention it deserves if you want to be effective in producing a desired result in as little time as possible. Why spend years accomplishing something that could be done in a matter of months? You'll have time for fun later, but not now. Your every waking moment, no matter where you are or what you are doing, the core of your thinking should always revolve around what is uppermost on your agenda until its fulfillment.

Keep the bigger picture at the forefront of your mind, and don't squander away your time. Be discriminating when it comes to how you spend your time and who you spend it with. Obviously your family is important. Quality time needs to be spent with them. And really, these two things—work and family—are where the bulk of your time is spent.

You should always know what you should be doing with your time. But how? Well, first you need to assess your overall situation, and based upon that assessment, it will dictate for you what you should or should not be doing. Time always dictates the agenda. When your actions are in accords with what time dictates, you will win. If not, you will lose. Knowing this alone will cover a multitude of things and will never cause you to veer off course. Being able to read time on this level is something many are not able to do on their own. Learn to do this, and anything you do will be a success.

* **Key Points:**
    a. By thinking beyond the present moment, no matter how pleasurable or painful, you will never be distracted.

b. Prioritize, don't take on too many tasks at a time, and limit unnecessary commitments.
c. Avoid unnecessary and involuntary idleness.
d. Take the time to recharge, rejuvenate, and recuperate; otherwise, you will suffer from burnout and fatigue.
e. Good planning is important in managing your time effectively.
f. Time always dictates the agenda.

Card 51: Time, Place, Space Dynamic

Time – The measured or measurable period during which an action, process, or condition exists or continues.

Place – Physical environment or surroundings.

Space – A boundless, three-dimensional extent in which objects and events occur and have relative position and direction. Physical space independent of what occupies it.

Dynamic – An underlying cause of change or growth.

*Concept/Objective: There is no need to be confused about where you fit in. At any given point in time, there is a special place reserved just for you and you alone, unoccupiable by anyone else. Find it, and you are on your way. Don't, and you will continue to be like a leaf in the wind.

(Questions)
1. What is life?
2. Why is it that some results are incapable of being duplicated to the same extent and to the same degree as previous results of others?
3. Is it possible to be anyone other than yourself?

On one level, life is simple. On another level, it is filled with complexity. So too are human beings. Simple, yet complex. Sometimes we make things more difficult than what they are. This is due to being unaware of our aim and purpose, and where we fit in when it comes to this thing called life. When, in fact, if we learned just that, then things would be a whole lot better.

Many people are, in one way or another, bogged down with a multiplicity of fears. The realm of the unknown produces natural yet unnecessary fears, fears that restrict us from reaching our full potential, realizing our goals, or engaging in purposeful acts. And because we are without the knowledge of what life is, we will continue to be restricted every which way. I've come to realize that everything is a matter of perspective. How we look at something ultimately determines how we approach what is in front of us.

The only real obstacle in your way is yourself. No matter what outside forces are arrayed against you, once you harness and connect with that part of you that is of the Divine, you will then be limitless and unrestricted in all that you do. There exists no one method of doing things that works the same for everyone. You must discover that special place that is reserved specifically just for you. You have heard that no two things can occupy the same space at the same time. This is a physical fact that extends itself and is applicable to more than just the physical realm. There are also mental and spiritual dimensions at play here.

The uniqueness of the individual demands such existence. Just as there is a literal physical space that only you can occupy, there are pockets of thought that are exclusively yours and not anyone else's but yours to roam around in and dominate. There is a course through life that has been specifically carved out for you. Your journey is yours. Another person's journey is theirs. So, find your niche.

None of us will ever be able to duplicate someone else's success exactly, no matter how much we follow every step they took. There are many unknown factors that contributed to things unfolding a particular way for a particular individual in a specific time. The only way we can come close to the results of someone else is if as many of the factors and conditions that were present in the past exist presently. Again, it will never be repeated exactly. You are you. You bring something uniquely different to the table. Even if you are at the same place, interact with the same people, and do the same thing, it does not matter. Perhaps this is why there is an adage that says, "The same man never crosses the same river twice."

This is multi-layered and needs to be examined because there is a dimension to this that has proven to be detrimental to many. The laws of success are general and can work for all in different ways. At the root of this is timing, preparation, hard work, opportunity, and circumstance. However, what you achieve may not reach the heights of someone else. Or what you achieve can surpass someone else. Many try to duplicate past acts of others but wonder why they are unable to get the exact result, and yet others who do things differently get a similar result.

This, in my estimation, has a lot to do with the above five factors. The mystery shall be removed from your mind when you understand that just one of the above factors, the timing of a thing, for example, can have a dramatic effect on outcomes. And when you add one or more of the other factors, the outcomes or results are many.

No man crosses the same river twice. If you crossed over a river today, and you crossed it at a particular point, 10 years from now, if you crossed that same river, you are not the same person, and 10 years from now, the river is not the same at that point of entry. The bottom line is this: You can only be you. No one else. Your ultimate success and happiness are dependent upon living your best life as it unfolds to you.

However, if you do choose to follow the footsteps of someone, let it be of those who have achieved greatness. For if you don't get exactly what they have in the past, at least you will acquire something of significance. In these instances, some examples are not only deserving of our attention; they deserve to be imitated.

When it is all said and done, you will never be able to escape yourself, so it is best to find the real you that is buried deep within yourself and relish in the absolute fact that you have been created perfectly in an imperfect world with the potential to become perfect. Learn to master your own reality as you know it to be and as it is distinguished from that of others. You have been assigned a role to play in life; a station; a lot, if you will. At any given point in time, you have a place in space. This is the Time, Place, and Space Dynamic.

*** Key Points:**
    a. You have a specific aim and purpose in life
    b. Your journey is yours
    c. No man crosses the same river twice
    d. Master your own reality

Card 52: Modus Operandi

Modus Operandi – A usual way of doing something.

*Modus operandi is Latin for "method of operating," abbreviated "m.o."

Method – A procedure or process for attaining something. A systematic procedure or technique. A way, technique, or process of or for doing something.

Operate – To perform or function. To produce an appropriate effect.

Operation – Performance of a practical work or of something involving the practical application of principles or processes. A method or manner of functioning.

*Concept/Objective: Often, there is no method to our madness. We have no specific way or technique of pursuing or obtaining our goals, no systematic approach to get what we desire, and we wonder why we fail to acquire anything. Get out of the shadows of others. Develop your own methodology. Apply your own principles and processes. Your very own modus operandi.

(Questions)
1. In the realm of power, what is one of the main things that differentiates you from others?
2. Is there an "end all be all" modus operandi that fits all occasions?
3. When it is all said and done, what is the ultimate goal?

"My thoughts are not your thoughts, neither are your ways my ways...For as the heavens are higher than the earth, so are my ways higher than your ways, and my thoughts than your thoughts." (10)

Your methodology is what differentiates you from others and puts you on a level that is enviable. To achieve this status, your every move has to be made with sheer precision, a preciseness that is unrivaled and is filled with so much ambiguity that it boggles the minds of others. Try as they might, none will be able to figure you out, yet, they will marvel at how you seem to effortlessly accomplish things at a rate and in a manner that they only wish they could imitate. Learn to appreciate the wisdom in not what you do, but how you do it.

As a practitioner of power, you will undoubtedly rub a few people the wrong way; you will be misjudged, and people will always question your moves. If you move according to how other people feel, pay too much attention to external criticisms, or take the time out to explain to everyone why you do what you do, you won't be able to accomplish anything of significance or worthwhile. So don't be deterred by any of this; it is merely one of the many prices you will have to pay for greatness and effective action.

No, there is never any one set way of doing things. Your modus operandi is what it is; however, it must be as varied, as there are different happenings. Your overall m.o. may never change, per se, but how you accomplish anything will. The core of your thinking is essentially a certain way. Whether you are a pragmatist, an analyst, an idealist, a realist, or a synthesis—or any combination of any of them—you will bring that style of thinking to bear heavily upon your method of operation and how you function. You must weigh every aspect of an ordeal to formulate a sophisticated way in handling a situation or producing a desired result.

"The goal is to amass so much power that you can do what you want, when you want, and the world be damned." (3)

It's all about winning and coming out on top. Develop a method of operation that is unique to you, one that compliments your natural abilities. Do this, and you will surely be the victor. Never mimic the ways of someone else. What works for them may not work for you. This does not mean that you can't extract something from them that will resurrect your dormant qualities. The only value in bringing this up is because we have a tendency to neglect our own capabilities while lauding those of others. Any excess in this area will only keep us stagnated and at a considerable distance from reaching our own goals.

There will always be advantages and disadvantages. By developing a set modus operandi, you can now be predicted, unless of course you elevate your thoughts and operate on a higher level of mind. Ordinarily, if your movements are always linear, then your patterned behavior and movements can be measured. But because your movements are governed by a higher law that has been exposed to you on the level of mind you now operate from, which is hidden from others, you will profoundly confound all observers. People will see your results, but they will never quite know how you arrived there.

When you function like this, things may appear sporadic, like you are all over the place, but you are not; it's just that what others see as unorthodox is really quite pragmatic, normal, and rational to you. Your analytics may throw people off. You can live with that. As long as you put thought behind what you do and develop a way of doing things that works for you, then everything else is irrelevant. If your ends are achieved, at little to no adverse cost, then you must have done something right. Your results speak for themselves.

Develop your own method of doing things. Never allow others to set you on a course or move in a way that suits them. Whatever you do, if it jives with you and there is no internal voice that speaks against your actions, then continue to do what you do. Be methodical. Operate effectively. Once you do this, you will be surgical in all that you do. Just know that your m.o. is your signature; make it as ineligible as possible. Others may know you were present because of your signature, mark, or particular way of doing something, but beyond that, nothing; your moves will be unimpeded.

*** Key Points:**
   a. It is not what you do, but how you do it that really matters.
   b. Don't worry about rubbing people the wrong way, being misjudged, or having your moves questioned.
   c. Actions have always spoken louder than words.
   d. Develop a method of operation that is unique to you; one that compliments your natural abilities.
   e. Elevate your thoughts and operate on a higher-level mind, where your moves are dictated by a more superior law.
   f. Your m.o. is your signature; make it as ineligible as possible.

Conclusion

This book evolved, in many respects, from its initial purpose. Other factors came into play that had to be considered and incorporated as this writing began to unfold and gain traction. I would consider this writing, as it is, an abridged version. So much more needs to be explained, and so much more ground needs to be covered. I do intend to work on the unabridged version sometime in the future when my circumstances put me in a much better position to provide a more comprehensive writing that will offer mor¬e information and give even greater clarity to the reader.

I made every attempt to be as clear as possible in the general way the various principles were explained. I did this with the goal of reaching a broader range of people, while at the same time staying as close as possible to the original intent I had in mind. These expressed thoughts are products of many years of studying and learning, a lot of trial and error, and plenty of experience in the form of disappointments, setbacks, and dissatisfaction.

It is my hope that the many people from whatever walk of life they may be from will have benefited from this writing and that you approached the subject matter with a sober mind and in the proper context, both of which can only be right or proper according to you.

I offer absolutely no apologies, however, for elements in this book that may be seen as dark, nor do I offer an apology for the various topics touched on in this book and the manner they were touched on that may go against the grain of what you think or believe to be true, right, or proper. Simply take a hold what you are drawn to and can extract from that can help you in some way.

It is my position that being void of knowledge of any kind is a crippling thing. There are many people who continue to be deprived of the main essentials of life because they are deprived of certain kinds or types of knowledge, those who have loss all hope of a better condition and have simply adjusted their minds to living their life as it is. So unfortunate. No one needs to have the avenues to the necessities of life closed off to them without realizing that there is a way to change their condition.

This change can be as small or as great as you need or want it to be. Each of us has it within us to be and do whatever we choose to be and do. All we must do is shift our way of looking at ourselves, others, and the world around us. And then muster up that reservoir of power that is hidden deep within each of us.

As much as this writing was written with so

many others in mind, it was also written for me. There were, and still are, many things that I am dealing with that are impeding me from living a more fulfilled life, one without certain constraints. I looked within and tried to produce a roadmap or blueprint that would help guide me through the many challenges I face daily, and this is what I attempted to share with each reader of this book. I discovered that self-motivation of all the forms of being motivated is perhaps the most powerful because it can push you in ways no outside force can.

Ultimately, no one will ever do for you what you can do for you, so why waste time sitting around hoping and wishing that a miracle will descend upon you without you doing something to help bring that blessing into your life? You would be surprised how far a little effort will get you, and what it can eventually bring into your life. If any of us continue to do nothing, how can we expect something to come from nothing? Nothing in; nothing out. At least with something, you have the potential to produce something. I have no doubt that each reader has what it takes to change or do whatever they desire, but sometimes, all we need is a little nudge. That's all this book is: something to nudge you along. I can say with certainty that it has nudged me. I pray that it has nudged you as well.

Bibliography
1. Classics of Strategy and Counsel; Thomas Cleary, Copyright © 2001
2. 48 Laws of Power; Robert Green, Copyright © 1998
3. The Art of Seduction; Robert Green, Copyright © 2001
4. Influence; Robert Cialdini, Copyright © 2006
   Thick Face, Black Heart; Chin-ning Chu, Copyright © 1992
5. The Asian Mind Game; Chin-ning Chu, Copyright © 1991
6. The Prince; Niccolo Machiavelli, Copyright © 1532
7. The Godfather; Mario Puzzo, Copyright © 1969
8. Rule by Secrecy; Jim Marrs, Copyright © 2000
9. Hoy Bible; King James Version, Copyright © 1970
10. Holy Qur'an; Maulana Muhammad, Copyright © 1999
11. The Black Book; The Executives, Copyright © 2014
12. The Secret; Rhonda Byrne, Copyright © 2006, 2016
13. Merriam Webster Collegiate Dictionary (Eleventh Edition); Principal Copyright © 2003
14. Merriam Webster's Vocabulary Builder (Second Edition); Mary Wood Cornog, Copyright © 2010

Upcoming Books by the Author

The Master's Deck II: Reloaded
The Hand that Rocks the Cradle